Ethics and Values in Social Work

Sarah Banks

First published 1995 by
MACMILLAN PRESS LTD
Houndmills, Basingstoke, Hampshire RG21 2XS
and London
Companies and representatives
throughout the world

ISBN 0–333–60918–2 hardcover
ISBN 0–333–60919–0 paperback

A catalogue record for this book is available
from the British Library.

10   9   8   7
04   03   02   01   00

Printed in Malaysia

To past and present community and youth work and social work students at Durham and York

Contents

List of Figures and Tables

Figures

Tables

Acknowledgements

The main stimulus for writing this book has been the dialogue and discussion generated through teaching ethics to trainee social workers, both at Durham and especially the many cohorts of York University Master of Social Work students.

I would like to thank the social workers who were prepared to discuss their ethical dilemmas with me – particularly trainee social workers from the Universities of York and Durham, and social workers from County Durham Social Services Department. I am also grateful to the Social Services Departments of Durham, Newcastle and Sunderland for providing me with documentation, and to the International Federation of Social Workers and the professional associations across the world that sent copies of their ethical codes. Many colleagues have offered encouragement and been prepared to discuss aspects of the book with me including Margaret Bell, Tim Bond, Lorna Durrani, Umme Imam, Juliet Koprowska, Kate Leonard, Una McCluskey, Audrey Mullender, Alf Ronnby, Muriel Sawbridge, Mark Smith and Bill Williamson. I have also benefited from Jo Campling's enthusiastic support, and the helpful comments of two anonymous referees.

Finally, I would like to thank my colleagues at Durham University for giving me space to complete a large part of the book during a period of research leave, Ken Fairless for his continuous support and encouragement and Fred Banks for first pointing me in the direction of moral philosophy.

SARAH BANKS

Introduction

The current context of social work

The occupation of social work is currently in a period of change – both in Britain and many other Western countries – as the role of the state as a direct provider of services declines, resources for welfare reduce and new styles of management and accountability are introduced. This makes it both difficult to look at the ethics and values of social work (because old values may be becoming irrelevant and new ones beginning to emerge) but also particularly important. Social work has always been a difficult occupation to define because it has embraced work in a number of different sectors (public, private, independent, voluntary), a multiplicity of different settings (residential homes, area offices, community development projects) with workers taking on a range of different tasks (caring, controlling, empowering, campaigning, assessing, managing) for a variety of different purposes (redistribution of resources to those in need, social control and rehabilitation of the deviant, prevention or reduction of social problems). This diversity, or 'fragmentation' as some have called it, is currently increasing, which raises the question of whether the occupation can retain the rather tenuous identity it was seeking to develop in the 1970s and 1980s (Langan 1993).

In such a climate of fragmentation, there are some who argue that it is the values of social work that should hold it together. Yet the values traditionally stated – user self-determination, acceptance, non-judgementalism, confidentiality, for example – are neither unique to social work, nor do they seem to be complete for social work. Similar statements of values or ethical principles are made for medicine, nursing, and counselling, for example. It is precisely because these values are so broad-ranging that they can encompass the variety of tasks and settings

1

which come under the umbrella of 'social work'. They are relevant to the 'caring professional' who is in a relationship of trust with a service user in need of help. Yet this description has never adequately characterised social work, which is also about controlling people in the interests of social order. So, not only do the traditional social work values fail to characterise social work uniquely, they also fail to encompass social work itself completely. Other values also seem relevant, such as fairness in the distribution of resources and the promotion of the public good. As local authority social work changes, with the emphasis less on the individual helping relationship and more on the distribution of resources and on social control, this is becoming more apparent. Probation officers and local authority social workers who are involved in the criminal justice system, community care, child protection and mental health are finding themselves increasingly working to legal and agency procedures and guidelines and hence ethical issues around justice and fairness are prominent. Whereas some of the new specialist services that are being set up largely in the voluntary sector, such as child advocacy or AIDS/HIV counselling, can operate more easily within the traditional casework value system which emphasises user self-determination (or its modern development, 'empowerment') and the rights and welfare of the individual user.

Terminology: 'social workers' and 'users'

The term 'social worker' is used in this book to refer to people who are paid in a professional capacity to undertake the tasks of counselling and/or social care planning as defined by the Barclay Report (1982, pp. xiv–xv). According to the report:

> By **counselling** we mean the process (which has often been known as 'social casework') of direct communication and interaction between clients and social workers, through which clients are helped to change, or to tolerate, some aspects of themselves or their environment. . .   .
> **Social care planning** covers plans designed to solve or alleviate existing problems and plans which aim to prevent the development

of social problems in the future or to create or strengthen resources
to respond to those which do arise.

These activities may be carried out by people who are not social
workers (volunteers, family members, other welfare professionals),
but it would be expected that all those calling themselves social
workers should be able to carry out, or organise the carrying out of,
such functions (ibid, p. 34). However, since the Barclay Report was
written, the roles of counselling and social care planning have
become more distinct, with many workers specialising much more
in one than the other. Is this book equally relevant to a care manager, an approved mental health social worker, a residential social
worker, a family therapist, a probation officer or a community
social worker? The answer is 'yes' insofar as they all regard themselves as social workers. Indeed many of the issues covered are
generic – including discussion of the professional code of ethics.
However, insofar as the context in which people work is regarded
as important (and I believe it is in relation to ethical and value
issues), then inevitably this book cannot take account of all the
different types of work settings and their impact on social workers'
values. It is mainly concerned with the ethical problems and
dilemmas faced by social workers working face-to-face, or organ-
ising care for individual users, rather than those faced by managers
of social workers or developers of services and communities.

I have tended to adopt the term 'user' to refer to the people
who use social work services. I prefer this to 'customer' or
'consumer' as these terms have connotations of choice and
market-based relationships which are not necessarily appropriate
in social work. Occasionally the term 'client' is used, as this was
until recently in common usage and much of the social work
literature, including the codes of ethics, uses this term. I have
tended to use 'she' when I am referring to a social worker
instead of the more cumbersome 'he/she'.

Terminology: 'ethics' and 'values'

It is also important to clarify the terms in the title of the book –
'ethics' and 'values'. Strictly speaking ethics is the study of morals

(the norms of behaviour people follow concerning what is right or wrong, good or bad). This is sometimes known as moral philosophy, which may comprise analysis of how we use or what we mean by terms such as 'good' or 'right' (meta-ethics) or the devising of actual systems of morality prescribing what people ought to do (normative ethics). However, the term is often used interchangeably with 'morals' to mean rules/norms of conduct concerning what is right/wrong and good/bad (as in 'code of ethics', for example). Because this is such a common usage of the term ethics, it will be used in this book in both of these senses.

The term 'values' is equally problematic. 'Social work values', 'the value-base of social work', 'social work as a value-laden activity' are all common phrases in the social work literature. Yet what is meant by 'the values of social work'? 'Values' is one of those words that tends to be used rather vaguely and has a variety of different meanings. In everyday usage, 'values' is often used to refer to one or all of religious, moral, political or ideological principles, beliefs or attitudes. In the context of social work, however, it seems frequently to be used to mean: a set of fundamental moral/ethical principles to which social workers are/should be committed. According to the Central Council for Education and Training in Social Work (CCETSW 1989, p. 15) such values include a commitment to 'the value and dignity of individuals' and 'the right to respect, privacy and confidentiality' for example. For the purpose of this discussion, while noting that the term 'values' is used in many different and conflicting ways, I will use it to refer to the fundamental moral/ethical principles of social work. Other commentators on social work ethics use the terminology differently (e.g. Levy 1993). The reason for including both 'ethics' and 'values' in the title of the book is that 'ethics' in its first meaning emphasises that the book is very much about *the study and analysis* of what is regarded as good or bad, right or wrong in social work practice.

Rationale and aims of the book

The discussion above suggests that it is both timely and difficult to explore the nature of the ethical and value issues inherent in social work practice. It is timely not just because the old values are under threat, but also because social workers themselves are increasingly under moral attack from the press and public for the outcomes of their actions. Recent controversies over the handling of child abuse cases, for example, raise ethical questions about the duties and rights of social workers, and the extent to which they should be blamed if a child dies, or if children are removed from their families unnecessarily. Many social workers feel a sense of guilt and anxiety when having to make a difficult ethical decision. While such feelings are inevitable for anyone who makes difficult decisions and has a sense of moral responsibility, should social workers take all the blame for bad outcomes? One of the purposes of this book is to encourage social workers to be clear about their own value positions, and hence to reduce some of the unnecessary feelings of guilt, blame and anxiety in making difficult ethical decisions.

In the course of collecting material for this book, I have found that when social workers are asked to describe ethical dilemmas in their practice, there is never any shortage of examples, and there is no need even to define what is meant by an 'ethical dilemma'. If we do define what is meant by the term 'ethical dilemma' – a choice between two equally unwelcome alternatives relating to human welfare – then it is immediately apparent that the occurrence of ethical dilemmas in social work is serious and common. There is never any shortage of cases where the rights of parents have to be balanced against the rights of children or the social worker's duty to the agency conflicts with a duty to the user, for example.

There are no easy answers to the ethical problems and dilemmas in social work practice. It is not possible (or desirable) to produce a rulebook which would enable social workers easily and quickly to resolve these dilemmas. Even if it were, the resolution of the dilemma will still entail making a choice between two unwelcome alternatives, perhaps by careful consideration and deciding that one alternative is less unwelcome than the other. Having made the choice, the impact of the dilemma does not go away; for even the least unwelcome alternative is still unwelcome. This is where some of the main stresses for social workers lie; not just in having to make difficult choices and decisions, but having to take responsibility for the unwelcome nature or outcomes of the decisions. For example:

> there is a 10-year-old boy whose parents are still barely able to control him after a lot of support from the social worker and other agencies. Should the social worker recommend that the boy be removed from the parental home which would go against the wishes of the parents and the boy and risk further disruptive behaviour as a result of the move, or should she recommend that he should stay at home which is contrary to the demands coming from neighbours and the school and risks further violent and disruptive behaviour towards other children and neighbours?

Both solutions have unwelcome consequences. The process of investigation, noting the legal and moral rights of different parties, the risks involved in both courses of action, and taking into account the legal and procedural responsibilities of the social worker is a complex one. Whatever course of action is taken, somebody's rights may be compromised and some of the consequences may be unwelcome.

The aim of this book is not to tell social workers how to make such choices – because I believe that would be both impossible and undesirable. It is impossible because of the complexity of social work decision-making; no rulebook could cover the variety of situations. It would be undesirable because it would suggest that social workers would simply have to follow the prescribed rules applying in each case and could in effect abrogate their individual responsibility for decision making. Rather, the book aims to encourage critical thinking and reflection through exploring what is the nature of the ethical problems and dilemmas in social work, how and why they arise, and what might be some alternative ways of tackling them according to different ethical theories and approaches. Through gaining a clearer understanding of what the problems and dilemmas are about, hopefully social workers can decide where they stand on some of the important ethical issues in the work and will have more confidence in justifying the decisions they have made, and may feel less obliged to take the blame for the inevitable unwelcome outcomes of social work intervention.

At the end of some of the chapters exercises have been included which can be used by readers to focus their thoughts around particular issues, or by tutors/facilitators teaching or working with groups of social workers. Case studies from social work practitioners have also been used, mainly in chapter 7, to illustrate how ethical problems and dilemmas arise and can be tackled in practice. Details of the cases and all names of people involved have been changed to preserve anonymity.

1

Ethical Issues in Social Work

There is general agreement amongst social work practitioners
and academics that questions of ethics, morals and values are an
inevitable part of social work. The majority of social workers,
when asked, have no difficulty in offering examples of ethical
problems and dilemmas. The literature of social work is also
very clear: 'Moral issues haunt social work', says Jordan (1990,
p. 1); according to Pinker 'social work is, essentially, a moral
enterprise' (Pinker 1990, p. 14); and the Central Council for
Education and Training in Social Work (CCETSW) states:
'Competence in social work requires the understanding and
integration of the values of social work' (CCETSW 1989, p. 15).

This chapter will explore what is the nature of the ethical
issues inherent in social work, and how and why questions of
ethics arise. It will also consider the guilt and anxiety felt by
social workers and whether the blame allocated to them
for outcomes of what are essentially moral decisions is
justified.

Moral decision-making

Much of social work is concerned with making decisions about
how to act in particular cases; for example, whether to commit a
confused woman to hospital against her will. This involves
making moral decisions or judgements. One such judgement
might be: 'it is morally wrong to commit this woman to hospital
against her will'. The view taken in this book about the nature of

moral judgements (modified from Banks 1990, p. 92) can be summarised as follows:

1. Moral judgements are about *human welfare* – for example, the promotion of human happiness or the satisfaction of needs (Norman 1983, pp. 225–32; Warnock 1967, pp. 48–72). What counts as a 'human need' will be relative to a particular society, or ideological belief system and will change over time.
2. Moral judgements entail *action*, that is they are prescriptive (Hare 1952; 1963). If a social worker makes the moral judgement that the woman suffering from confusion ought not to be committed to hospital against her will, then the worker should be prepared to act on this, which might include making plans for her to stay at home and being prepared to argue the case to her family and to professional colleagues.
3. A moral judgement should be *universalisable*, in the sense that it should apply to all people in similar circumstances. The social worker should make the same moral judgement about another confused woman, unless it could be demonstrated that the situation was significantly different.
4. It makes sense to ask people to *justify* their moral judgements. They may do so with reference to particular relationships and responsibilities or to some general moral judgements or principles within their particular system of morality. In this case, the social worker might refer to the principle that 'all individuals have a right to decide for themselves what they want to do' (self-determination). This in turn might be justified with reference to the principle that 'all persons should be respected as rational and self-determining beings'. Ultimately a stage is reached where no further justification can be given and certain beliefs about the nature of human welfare and needs have to be taken as given.

Not all philosophers would accept these statements (for a more detailed discussion of different theories of ethics see Hudson 1970) and in chapter 2 we discuss an 'ethic of care' (Tronto

1993) which challenges the view of morality as based on rational justification with reference to principles.

The ethical, the technical and the legal

Frequently in the social work literature values are distinguished from knowledge, and ethical/moral issues from legal and technical matters. Such distinctions can be useful, as long as it is not implied that knowledge can be value-free, or that legal and technical decisions can be made without recourse to ethics. We might say, 'it is essentially a legal question whether to detain this person in hospital under the Mental Health Act'. Yet, as Braye and Preston-Shoot point out (1992, p. 39) the law is rarely clear, and has to be interpreted by the social worker. The Mental Health Act 1983 talks of: 'mental disorder of a nature or degree which warrants the detention of the patient in a hospital – in the interest of his [*sic*] own health or safety or with a view to the protection of others'.

The law tells us that if we make the technical (and ethical) judgement that the disorder is such that it is in the patient's interest to be detained in hospital, then we have the legal powers to do so. The law does not tell us what we ought to do, just what we can do. The law itself reflects certain values and norms in society – some of which we may regard as immoral, for example immigration laws. Most decisions in social work involve a complex interaction of ethical, political, technical and legal issues which are all interconnected. Our ethical principles or values will influence how we interpret the law.

Giving another example, we might say, 'it is a technical matter to decide whether this person is eligible for a disabled car parking badge'. We assess the person according to the defined criteria and make a decision using our professional skill and judgement. We might only judge that moral issues were involved if we had to consider whether we ought to give the person a permit, although she did not quite meet the criteria. This is a helpful distinction between the technical and the ethical. However, a decision might be regarded as a technical one not because only technical questions of measurement and assessment were involved, but because the social worker chose to see it in that way – as he/she might if it were a relatively straightforward case which did not present any ethical problems or dilemmas. The process itself, assessing needs for a parking permit, is not devoid of ethical content. The criteria of need which determine who should get permits will be based on ethical judgements about social duties to reduce some of the disadvantages caused by disability, or how to distribute a scarce resource efficiently and fairly, for example. The social worker may judge that the criteria are not fair or do not result in resources being allocated to the most needy people.

In the light of the discussion above, it may be useful to distinguish between ethical issues, ethical problems and ethical dilemmas as follows:

- **ethical issues** – pervade the social work task (including what appear to be 'legal' or 'technical' matters) in that social work takes place in the context of the welfare state premised on principles of social justice and public welfare and the social worker has professional power in the relationship with the user. So, although deciding whether to give a parking permit to a person with a disability in a case which is straightforward may not involve the social worker in agonising over a moral dilemma, it is not devoid of ethical content.
- **ethical problems** – arise when the social worker sees the situation as involving a difficult moral decision, for example, when she has to turn down the application of a very needy person because this person does not quite fit the criteria.
- **ethical dilemmas** – occur when the social worker sees herself as faced with a choice between two equally unwelcome alternatives which may involve a conflict of moral principles and it is not clear which choice will be the right one. For example, should she bend the criteria for issuing parking permits in order to help a very needy person, or stick to the rules and refuse a permit to someone who really needs it. She is faced with a conflict between the interests of this individual and the public interest in having rules and criteria which apply to everyone.

Thus what is a technical matter for one person (simply applying the rules) may be an ethical problem for another (a difficult decision, but it is clear what decision should be made) or a dilemma for a third person (there appears to be no solution). It depends on how each person sees the situation, how experienced they are at making moral decisions and how they prioritise their ethical principles.

What are the ethical issues in social work?

In talking to qualified and trainee social workers there seem to be three main types of issues involved, which frequently result in ethical problems and dilemmas:

- *Issues around individual rights and welfare* – a user's right to make her own decisions and choices; the social worker's responsibility to promote the welfare of the user.
- *Issues around public welfare* – the rights and interests of parties other than the user; the social worker's responsibility to her employing agency and to society; the promotion of the greatest good of the greatest number of people.
- *Issues around inequality and structural oppression* – the social worker's responsibility to challenge oppression and to work for changes in agency policy and in society.

Any categorisation is obviously artificial, and does not do justice to the complexity of the issues within each category, and the overlap between them. Frequently there are conflicts between rights, responsibilities and interests both within and between these categories. However, this framework may be a useful starting point for exploring issues of values and ethics in social work practice. Quotations from three social workers talking about their practice may illuminate our discussion.

1. *Rights/welfare of the individual*

A social worker talking about an 80-year-old woman recently referred to the Social Services Department by a local hospital after a fall at home said:

> It was difficult to know how far to try to persuade or even coerce Mrs Brown to accept the offer of a home help or whether just to leave her alone and hope she would manage to survive.

Here the focus of the worker's concern is the user's welfare. The social worker wants to respect Mrs Brown's own choices about how to live her life, yet the worker also wants to ensure Mrs Brown feeds herself properly and is checked regularly in case she falls again. There is a conflict between the promotion of the user's welfare and the user's rights to make her own choices.

2.   *Public welfare*

A residential social worker spoke about Sally, a 12-year-old girl who had recently come into care because her parents felt her behaviour was out of control. She had been having sexual relations with a 50-year-old man who supplied her with money in return for sexual favours:

> the police were near to catching the man, and asked staff to lift restrictions on Sally leaving the unit in the hope of catching him in the act. Should we have refused because we were allowing Sally to put herself at risk, or was catching the culprit and preventing further risk to herself and other girls a priority?

The social worker sees that it will be in the best interests of everyone if this man is caught, yet feels uneasy about using the young girl in this way, both because of the deception involved, and the responsibility if any harm comes to Sally when she is allowed out. This is a case of deciding whether the public interest in catching the man outweighs the deception involved and the short-term risk to the girl.

3.   *Structural oppression*

A social worker visited a travelling family who had requested that their children attend a local playgroup. When she arrived to discuss how to provide financial support, she was told that the children had been refused access on the grounds that it may cause other local families to remove their children and hence threaten the viability of the playgroup. During the visit the social worker noticed that the children had been playing with an electric fire and plugs while the worker was talking to their parents:

> I realised that in another situation I may well have challenged the parents in allowing their children to play with such a dangerous appliance. Given that I felt they were being treated very shabbily by the wider community, I found it very difficult to challenge any of the ways in which they cared for their children.

The social worker is aware that the travellers are being discriminated against by the local community, and by wider society. She does not want to collude in this, but is not sure how to react. This is a case of a social worker recognising she is working with members of an oppressed group, not wishing to oppress them further by challenging their standards of childcare, yet concerned about the safety of children.

The descriptions above have simplified the issues arising in each case. In many cases issues in all three categories arise, and some of the dilemmas workers face are about balancing different ethical principles – different sets of rights, interests and value-commitments. Social work is a complex activity, with many layers of duties and responsibilities (for example, to one's own moral integrity, to the user, to the agency and to society). These often conflict and have to be balanced against each other. There are no easy answers to questions such as these. They are part of the everyday life of social workers. Some will handle them more easily than others – depending on experience, moral sensitivity and their own value positions. In the following sections we will explore how and why questions of ethics are an integral part of social work practice.

Social work as a human services profession

Social work can be regarded as a 'human services' profession along with medicine and the law. The social worker has special knowledge and expertise and must be trusted by the user to act in his/her best interests. The relationship between social worker and user is an unequal one, in that the social worker is more powerful. Social work, therefore, along with law, medicine, nursing, counselling, and other similar professions has a code of ethics which is designed, among other things, to protect the user from exploitation or misconduct. Some commentators describe the social worker–user relationship as a 'fiduciary' one – that is, based on a relationship of trust (Levy 1976, p. 55 ff; Kutchins 1991).

While many of the similarities between social work and professions like law and medicine are sound, there are several ways in which social work is different. Some have argued that social work is a 'semi-profession', partly because the individual autonomy of social workers is more limited than that of doctors and lawyers. Many social workers are either directly or indirectly employed by local authorities; they have a social control function and therefore their primary aim is not straightforwardly to work in the best interests of the user. The social worker also functions as part of the welfare state which is itself based on contradictory principles.

Social work and the welfare state

Social work is part of a state organised and funded system for distributing goods and services to meet certain types of social needs of individuals, families, groups and communities and to cure, contain or control behaviour that is regarded as socially problematic or deviant. It is part of a welfare state which organises and funds a range of other social services, including education, health, social security and housing, and public services such as police, army, roads and refuse collection (Spicker 1988, pp. 74–5). These are collective services which, in principle, benefit the whole community. However, social services are often regarded as different from public services in that they are seen as a means of transferring resources to people who are dependent – through sickness, old age, childhood, unemployment, disability, for example. Welfare states are allied to capitalist economies and have a redistributive role through taxation, compulsory social insurance and direct provision of services. They can be seen as compensating for defects in the market system in the allocation of goods and services.

Many commentators analyse the nature of the welfare state in terms of contradictions. Marshall (1972) saw the tensions inherent in welfare-capitalism between the values of social justice and equality as opposed to the competitive individualism of the market, though he recognised that the aim of the welfare state is not to remove inequality of income, rather it is to eradicate poverty and give everyone equal status as citizens in society. According to O'Connor (1973, p. 6) the welfare state has two contradictory functions in capitalist societies – that of accumulation (enabling private capital to remain profitable) and legitimation (of the existing economic and social order). Moon succinctly summarises the contradictory principles upon which the welfare state is based as follows:

> The welfare state embraces the market, but at the same time seeks to limit and control it; it incorporates ideas of rights, especially rights to property and the fruits of one's labor, but asserts a right to welfare, a right to have one's basic needs met; it is based on a conception of the person as a responsible agent but recognises as well that many of the conditions of one's life are due to circumstances beyond one's control; it is premised upon sentiments of sociability and common interest, but its very success may undermine those sentiments; it seeks to provide security, but embraces as well a commitment to liberty (Moon 1988, p. 12).

Moon suggests that this is one reason why the welfare state appears to be so vulnerable to criticism. Others might disagree that it is the contradictions per se that make it vulnerable (Offe 1984, ch. 5) but there is no doubt that at the present time the whole concept of the welfare state – its aims, its functions, its methods and its outcomes – are the subject of questioning and criticism from various quarters (both right and left). The economic recession of the mid-1970s gave rise to a sustained critique of the welfare state from right-wing politicians and theorists, and this has been reinforced by the recession of the late 1980s/early 1990s. First, the burden of taxation and regulation imposed on capital is claimed to serve as a disincentive to investment. Secondly, welfare benefits and the collective power of trades unions amount to a disincentive to work. The argument has also been made that family values and responsibilities, a sense of community and moral obligation may, in fact, be undermined by the welfare state. Criticisms from the left tend to focus on the ineffectiveness and inefficiency of the welfare bureaucracies, which have done little to redistribute income between classes and do not tackle the fundamental causes of poverty and unemployment. Feminist and anti-racist critiques have been increasingly vocal as many aspects of the welfare state have been shown to reinforce gender and race stereotyping, discrimination and oppression. The welfare state is also seen as a repressive instrument of social control (through individualising problems and distinguishing between the deserving and undeserving).

This discussion of social work as part of the welfare state is important as it helps us understand how some of the ethical issues are inherent in the role of the social worker. As part of the welfare state it is based on contradictions and societal ambivalence. Social work contributes towards expressing society's altruism (care) and enforcing societal norms (control); it champions individual rights as well as protects the collective good. Social workers are regarded as wimps (caring for those who do not deserve it) and as bullies (wielding too much power over individuals and families).

Blame and guilt in social work

The position of social workers in the welfare state not only places them at the heart of the contradictions of the welfare state itself, but also leads to them bearing the brunt of the blame for certain unpalatable societal problems such as child abuse. One of the most publicised areas of social work is child protection. In this context, if a bad outcome occurs, social workers usually get the blame. A bad outcome can be either that children left at home suffer or die, or that children are removed from home unnecessarily. Franklin (1989) demonstrates how the press portray social workers either as indecisive wimps who fail to protect children from death, or as authoritarian bullies who unjustifiably snatch children from their parents. Either way, the social workers are to blame. As Franklin comments:

> Press reporting of child abuse, paradoxically, rarely focuses upon the abuse of children. It quickly regresses into an attack on welfare professionals, particularly social workers who, in their turn, seem to have become a metaphor for the public sector (Franklin 1989, p. 1).

Social workers can be seen as symbols of the welfare state, simultaneously representing two of its much criticised facets – bungling inefficiency and authoritarian repression. Social workers, Franklin claims, seem to have a unique place among professionals in being regarded as culpable by the press for the fate of their users. This may be partly connected with the more ambivalent and morally charged role that social workers play in society. For example, doctors treat people who are sick; and sickness might be regarded as an unfortunate state which generally affects individuals through no fault of their own. Social workers are often working with people whom society regards as 'undeserving', idle, feckless or deviant. They have a control as well as a care function. It is their job to protect society from deviant or morally dangerous people; if they fail to do this job, they are committing a moral crime. Physical and sexual abuse of children, particularly by their parents, is a threat to social stability and the idea of the family as a good and caring setting. Child abuse in families, therefore, must not happen. It must either be prevented by social workers (and therefore barely exist) or not exist at all. Social workers' vilification by the press and public is partly due to their role as welfare professionals in a society that is ambivalent about the welfare state and also the particular role they play within the welfare state which includes both the care and control of people whom the family or other state agencies cannot help and who may be regarded as difficult or deviant.

Social workers tend feel that they should not always take the blame in cases where children are abused or die. The situation is complex: resource constraints mean that social workers cannot always provide the services required; decisions regarding how to handle children at risk are usually taken by inter-professional groups at case conferences and are a shared responsibility; assessing the nature of risk of child abuse is an uncertain art and even the most skilled and competent professionals who follow all the guidelines and procedures may find a child dies. Obviously if workers fail to follow the procedures correctly or neglect to carry out specified duties, then they are culpable. Yet if a worker does the best she can in the circumstances, surely she should not be blamed? This is certainly the line taken by Macdonald (1990) and seems to make sense to most social workers. However, it is not the view of Hollis and Howe, who claim that it is justifiable to blame social workers for bad outcomes (such as child deaths) even if they have done their well-intentioned best. Social workers must accept this as part of their role, which involves a high level of moral risk. They suggest that:

> the social worker would receive better sympathy, if her responsibility for bad outcomes was understood to be personal yet, at the same time, a function of the role rather than of self-evident personal incompetence (Hollis and Howe 1990, p. 548).

Their view, they suggest, helps explain why professional social workers are troubled by guilt even when they have done their best.

Hollis and Howe are, in a sense, putting social work decision-making back into the sphere of the moral, suggesting that the more comfortable retreat into the bureaucratic and technical (following procedures and making technical 'risk assessments') is not an appropriate response to public blame. Yet, in order to do this, is it necessary for Hollis and Howe to go so far as to say that social workers should always be blamed for a bad outcome? Their view depends upon accepting the premise that the outcomes of an action/decision determine the nature of the action/decision. If the child survives and thrives, the action was morally right; if the child dies, the action was morally wrong. It appears that such decisions are what Nagel would describe as 'decisions under uncertainty' (Nagel 1976, p. 143) where the overall moral judgement can shift from positive to negative depending on the outcome. While we might agree that the death of a child is a negative outcome, and that the social worker involved in the case might have made a technically wrong decision not to remove the child from the family, was it also a morally wrong decision? Surely not, if the social worker gained as much information as possible, assessed the risk and made the judgement that the risk to the child was low? We might even question whether the decision was 'technically' wrong. The social worker may have been right – the risk was one in 100 and the fact that this case was the one in a 100 does not prove the social worker wrong – one might say she was unlucky. Risk assessment in social work is not a precise, scientific or straightforward business. It might be the case that the technical decision is a 'decision under uncertainty', so we would, in fact, say that the social worker's assessment was correct or incorrect according to the outcome. However, to say that it is *morally* right or wrong according to the outcome is surely going too far? That social workers feel 'guilt' for a bad outcome is surely not surprising. Yet in the same way that my friends would tell me not to feel guilty for running over a young child who unexpectedly leapt out in front of my car, surely we would say the same to the social worker? We may torment ourselves by blaming ourselves and thinking 'if only I had reacted more quickly; if only I had visited the family an hour earlier' but what we should feel is regret, not guilt. I imagine Hollis and Howe would respond that the cases are not analogous. They liken, in fact, the social worker to the driver of a car who nevertheless drives knowing the brakes are faulty. If I had run over the child while driving with faulty brakes, then I would have been morally blameworthy.

According to Hollis and Howe, in taking on the job of social worker, the worker knows that she is being asked to drive a car with faulty brakes. Therefore she must expect and accept moral blame when bad outcomes occur (as they inevitably will). Yet this analogy does not capture the complexity of social work practice. Firstly, while this may not exonerate the social worker, it is important to note that it is not her job to service the car. Secondly, while she may be in the driving seat, there are plenty of others in the car map-reading, directing, and changing gear. Thirdly, while objective observers like Hollis and Howe may claim that the brakes are faulty, the rest of society regards such a state as the norm, and is certainly not prepared to pay to improve the brakes. If social workers take moral responsibility, they are, in effect, allowing others to scapegoat them and to avoid taking blame and hence to avoid recognising the variety of contributing factors that caused the child's death and the need to change some of these factors. Also, if social workers take the blame, they become personally and professionally undermined and stressed. To allow oneself to be blamed for outcomes of which many of the causes are outside one's control is debilitating and draining. It may be appropriate to take some responsibility, and hence blame, but certainly not all of it. The retreat into 'defensive' social work (following rules and procedures) becomes even more necessary and appealling as a survival strategy.

One of the purposes of this book is to enable social workers to gain an understanding of the nature of moral decision-making and hence to feel less guilt and blame for the outcomes of decisions and actions with which they are involved. Very often in connection with moral and ethical issues in social work (and indeed the caring professions generally) the term 'dilemma' is used. As has already been noted, a dilemma is usually defined along the lines of 'a choice between two equally unwelcome alternatives' – which seems to sum up quite well how it often feels to be a social worker in a 'no win' situation. For example, in a child protection case, if the child is removed from the family both the child and the mother will be unhappy and the child may have to spend some time in institutional care, which may be damaging. Yet if the child remains with the family, there is a chance that the child will suffer physical abuse from the father and may be injured or even die. The way to resolve the dilemma is to try to work out whether one of the alternatives is more unwelcome than the other and then act on that. Of course, we also need to try to work out how likely it is that each of the unwelcome outcomes will occur. We might decide that it is more unwelcome (indeed it would be tragic) for the child to die, than to be unhappy. But it is thought to be highly unlikely that the father will seriously injure or kill the child. So, on balance, it is decided to leave the child with the family. We know it is a risk – a moral risk as well as a technical one – which was why we described the situation as a dilemma. There are not welcome outcomes, only less unwelcome ones; when the choice is the lesser of two evils, whichever one chooses, it is an 'evil'. This is a constant problem for the social worker. If the social worker has carefully thought through all aspects of the dilemma, and made a decision to act in order to try to avoid the worst outcome, she has acted with moral integrity.

We will return to this important issue of the guilt and blame felt by social workers and will explore further how these can be counteracted at the end of the book, in the light of the more detailed discussion of ethical and value issues in the next few chapters.

Conclusions

In this chapter we have set the scene for our discussion of questions of ethics in social work. We have argued that the ethical problems and dilemmas are inherent in the practice of social work. The reasons for this arise from its role as a public service profession dealing with vulnerable users who need to be able to trust the worker and be protected from exploitation; also from its position as part of the welfare state which is itself based on contradictory aims and values (care and control; capital accumulation and legitimation; protection of individual rights and promotion of public welfare), which cause tensions, dilemmas and conflicts. The current 'crises' of the welfare state, which entail a questioning of both its legitimation function and its capital accumulation function are increasing the tensions and dilemmas for social workers, who very often find themselves the victims of media attacks and public blame. We argued that this blame is often unjustified and it is important that social workers understand both their role at the sharp end of the contradictions of the welfare state, and consider how moral decisions are actually made in social work, in order that they are not consumed by unnecessary guilt about the unfortunate, tragic, or unwanted outcomes of cases they have been involved in.

Exercise 1

Aims of the exercise – to encourage readers to identify ethical issues in their own practice and to reflect on and clarify their own ethical stance.

1. Briefly describe a situation/incident/event in your experience as a practitioner which raised ethical issues for you.
2. List the ethical issues.
3. What does your view of this situation/event tell you about the important values/ethical principles that underpin your practice as a social worker?

2

Social Work Values

This chapter will explore the philosophical foundations of the key values that have been traditionally stated as underpinning social work, and look at the extent to which recent developments in the policy and practice of social work are influencing the values of the profession.

Principles of the social worker–user relationship: Kantian approaches

Until recently, much of the literature on social work values and ethics has focussed on lists of principles about how the social worker ought to treat the individual user. Such lists are often adaptations or modifications of the seven principles developed by Biestek, an American Catholic priest, in the late 1950s (Biestek 1961). These principles have been surprisingly influential, especially given two factors. First, Biestek did not intend them as ethical principles per se. Indeed he seems to regard them primarily as principles for effective practice – instrumental to the social workers' purpose of 'helping the client achieve a better adjustment between himself and his [*sic*] environment' (Biestek 1961, p. 12). Secondly, his emphasis is primarily on the voluntary one-to-one casework relationship, where the user initiates the contact by coming to the agency and relates individually to a social worker. This is somewhat removed from the complexities of modern social work which include compulsory intervention within a statutory framework and work with families, groups and communities. However, since the principles have been so influential, it may be useful to summarise them here (adapted from Biestek 1961):

1. *Individualisation* is the recognition of each user's unique qualities, based upon the rights of human beings to be treated not just as a human being but as this human being.
2. *Purposeful expression of feelings* is the recognition of users' need to express their feelings (especially negative ones) freely. The caseworker should listen purposefully without condemnation and provide encouragement when therapeutically useful.
3. *Controlled emotional involvement* is the caseworker's sensitivity to users' feelings, an understanding of their meaning and a purposeful, appropriate response to them.
4. *Acceptance* entails the caseworker perceiving and dealing with users as they really are, including their strengths and weaknesses, congenial and uncongenial qualities, maintaining throughout a sense of their innate dignity and personal worth.
5. *Non-judgemental attitude* entails that it is not part of the casework function to assign guilt or innocence or degrees of user responsibility for causation of problems, although evaluative judgements can be made about the attitudes, standards or actions of users (that is, the caseworker does not judge users themselves, but their behaviour).
6. *User self-determination* is the recognition of the right and need of users to freedom in making their own choices and decisions in the casework process. Caseworkers have a duty to respect that need and help activate users' potential for self-direction. Biestek stresses, however, that users' rights to self-determination are limited by their capacity for positive and constructive decision-making, by civil and moral law and by the function of the agency.
7. *Confidentiality* is the preservation of secret information concerning the user which is disclosed in the professional relationship. Biestek describes confidentiality as based upon a basic right of users and as an ethical obligation for the social worker, as well as being essential for effective casework service. However, users' rights are not absolute and may be

Table 2.1 *Principles of the social work relationship*

Biestek's principles	Examples of their adoption/modification					
	Biestek (1961)	Moffet (1968)	Plant (1970)	CCETSW (1976)	Butrym (1976)	Ragg (1977)
Individualisation	*	*	*	*	*	*
Purposeful expression of feelings	*	*			*	*
Controlled emotional involvement	*				*	
Acceptance	*	*	*	*	*	
Non-judgemental attitude	*				*	
User self-determination	*	*	*	*	*	*
Confidentiality	*	*		*	*	
Respect for persons			*	*	*	*

limited by a higher duty to self, by rights of other individuals, the social worker, agency or community.

During the 1960s and 1970s many other theorists adopted modified versions of Biestek's list of principles, often with the addition of the ultimate or basic principle of 'respect for persons', as Table 2.1 demonstrates.

A key theme running through all these principles could be identified as *respect for the individual person as a self-determining being*. It is significant that the first principle in the list, and one which has also been taken on board by all the other writers noted in Table 2.1, is 'individualisation' the recognition of each user's unique qualities based upon the right of human beings to be treated as individuals with personal differences. The other important principle which has also been adopted by all the other writers is 'user self-determination' – recognition of users' rights to freedom in making their own decisions and choices. Many of the subsequent writers have, in fact, included in their lists the basic or ultimate principle of 'respect for persons' which, it has been argued, underpins social work ethics, and, indeed any system of moral thinking (Plant 1970). Although Biestek himself did not include this principle in his list, his principles are compatible with it. Before proceeding further, it is important to define some of the terms involved in this principle:

- *'person'* refers to beings who are capable of rational thought and self-determined action;
- *'rational'* means the ability to give reasons for actions;
- *'self-determining'* entails acting according to one's own choices and desires and having the ability to make decisions;
- *'respect'* can be regarded as an 'active sympathy' towards another human being (Downie and Telfer 1969; 1980).

This principle is derived from Kant, the eighteenth-century German philosopher, who formulated it as categorical imperative (i.e. a command that must be adhered to), one version of which is: 'So act as to treat humanity, whether in your own person or that of any other, never solely as a means but always also as an end' (Kant 1964, pp. 32–3).

By this he meant that we should treat others as beings who have ends (that is choices and desires), not just as objects or a means to our own ends. The individual person is intrinsically worthy of respect simply because she or he is a person, regardless of whether we like the person, whether she or he is useful to us or has behaved badly towards us. It can be seen how some of Biestek's principles directly follow from this ultimate principle – not just user self-determination, but also acceptance, non-judgementalism and confidentiality. Accepting a user as she is, rather then stereotyping or categorising is obviously part of respecting the innate worth and dignity of every human being. Similarly with non-judgementalism – the social worker should not judge the person as unworthy, evil or inadequate. Breaking confidence would violate the principle of respect for persons, because it would entail not respecting the user's wishes, treating her, perhaps, as a means to an end.

Commentators on social work ethics and values in the 1980s have tended to move away from the 'list approach' and from the focus solely on the nature of the social worker–user relationship. There are a number of reasons why the kind of list suggested by Biestek and others is unsatisfactory. First, such broad general principles can be interpreted variously, and there are confusions both within and between writers using the same terminology. McDermott (1975) indicates, for example, that the term self-determination is, in fact, defined persuasively in social work and that the favourable connotations of freedom from constraint are used to justify what amounts to a recommendation that the social worker should decide what users' real interests are and may be justified in promoting them against their will, a tendency which can be seen in the Biestek formulation. In fact, self-determination can mean all things to all people, from maintaining that each individual should be completely free to do whatever he or she wants (a version of negative freedom which might be associated with a form of Kantian philosophy based on respect for persons), to justifying fairly large-scale intervention from the state to enable individuals to become more self-determining or self-realising (a version of positive freedom which might be associated with Hegelian or Marxist ethics). Within social work, interpretations at the negative end of the spectrum would tend to advocate freedom from restraint unless another's interests are threatened; whereas on a more positive view, a further clause is often added, 'and/or unless the person's own interests are threatened'.

Similar problems regarding meaning arise for the principles of non-judgementalism, acceptance and confidentiality. For example, Stalley (1978) argues that non-judgementalism appears to be about refraining from making moral judgements about a person's character, yet at the same time, social workers have a responsibility to society to help users, and to maintain their own moral integrity by making moral judgements. This raises the question of where we draw the lines around these principles, which can only be answered in relation to other principles within a more systematic framework of moral beliefs and principles. This is complicated by the second difficulty arising from such lists of principles, namely, that very little indication is given of the status of the different principles. Some appear to be methods for effective practice (for example, purposeful expression of feelings), others might be regarded as professional standards (for example, confidentiality), others might be classified as general moral principles (such as self-determination) and one (respect for persons) has been characterised as the basic presupposition of any morality.

A third problem is caused by the fact that many writers do not rank the principles and no indication is given of what to do in cases of conflicting principles. We may well ask what criteria are to be used for judging between, say, promoting a user's self-determination at the expense of revealing a confidential secret? Some theorists do state, following Downie and Telfer (1969), that their sets of principles follow directly from one ultimate principle, respect for persons. If this were the case, then respect for persons could be referred to in cases of conflict. However, apart from Plant, and to some extent CCETSW (1976), little detail is given as to how respect for persons can actually be used to justify the other principles, nor how it can be used in actual moral decision-making to arbitrate between principles. While Downie and Telfer do articulate a moral system for social work based on respect for persons, they do not derive from it the kinds of principles suggested in Table 2.1 as relevant to social work. This may not be surprising, since these principles, if regarded as moral principles, are certainly not complete for social work. Indeed, as Biestek envisaged them they were more a set of principles for effective casework, focussing on the *content of the relationship* – how the individual user should be treated by the social worker. Insofar as moral matters were involved for Biestek, these centred around notions of individual rights/ liberties, rather than the questions of social justice and responsibility, which attention to the *context of the agency* and society generally would raise for the social worker.

The agency and societal context of social work: utilitarian dimensions

More recent writers on social work ethics have been critical of the lists of principles focussing on the individual worker–user relationship within a broadly Kantian ethical framework, pointing out that other types of moral principles also influence social work practice (Banks 1990; Clark with Asquith 1985; Horne 1987; Rhodes 1986). Social workers are not autonomous professionals whose guiding ethical principles are solely about respecting and promoting the self-determination of service users. They are employed by agencies, work within the constraints of legal and procedural rules and must also work to promote the public good or the well-being of society in general. Other types of ethical principles concerned with utility (promoting the greatest good) and justice (distributing the good(s) as widely and/or fairly as possible) are important. There may be conflicts between the rights or interests of different people – for example a parent and a child, a confused older man and his carer. Within a Kantian framework it is difficult to decide whose right to self-determination has priority. The Kantian approach also advocates always following one's duty no matter what the outcome. For example, lying is always wrong, because it would involve manipulating a person and failing to treat him/her with proper respect – even if by lying a life could be saved. Such an approach fails to take account of how social workers actually do behave. Very often they have to look to the consequences of their actions and weigh up which action would be least harmful/most beneficial to a particular user, and which action would benefit most people, or uses resources most efficiently. This kind of ethical theory has been termed 'utilitarianism'.

The basic idea of utilitarianism is very simple – that the right action is that which produces the greatest balance of good over evil (the principle of utility). However, so many philosophers have added so many qualifications and modifications to enable this doctrine to capture more and more of our ordinary conceptions of morality, that any discussion of what is known as utilitarianism becomes very complicated. First, Bentham and some recent philosophers equate the good with happiness (the sum of pleasures) and the bad with unhappiness (the sum of pains), espousing what has been called *hedonistic utilitarianism* (see Plamenatz 1966; Smart and Williams 1973). Whereas others, notably Mill, claim that the good consists of other things besides happiness (for example, virtue, knowledge, truth, beauty), a view known as *ideal utilitarianism* (Mill 1972). Secondly, some philosophers espouse what has been called *act utilitarianism*, which involves deciding the rightness of each action with reference directly to the principle of utility (Smart and Williams 1973). Others advocate *rule utilitarianism*, claiming that we do in fact use rules to speed up the process of moral reasoning and decision-making, and that the rules themselves are tested and justified with reference to the principle of utility (Downie 1971). For example, we adhere to the rule of promise-keeping despite the fact that on some occasions it might produce a greater balance of evil over good, because promise-keeping as a whole generally produces good.

However, so far the principle of utility has said nothing about whose good, that is, about the distribution of the good. If we could choose between an action which produced a large amount of good (let us assume we are talking about happiness) for two people and nothing for eight people, and an action which produced slightly less total happiness, but distributed it equally between ten people, would we choose the former? This led Bentham to introduce his proviso – everyone to count for one and no one for more than one, and to Mill's formulation of the principle of utility as the greatest good of the greatest number. Here we seem to have a principle against which conflicts between derived principles and rules (if we are rule utilitarians) or between particular actions (if we are act utilitarians) can be decided. However, as critics have pointed out, we now have two principles, in effect: utility (urging us to produce as much good as possible) and justice (as equality of treatment, urging us to distribute it as widely as possible), which themselves may conflict. As Raphael suggests, the most difficult conflicts in life are between these two principles: he gives the example of whether the government should give large grants to engineering students in the national interests (utility) or the same amount to each student for the sake of fairness (justice) (Raphael 1981).

A Kantian-utilitarian framework

The above discussions suggest that neither Kantian nor utilitarian theories of ethics can furnish us with one ultimate principle for determining the rightness and wrongness of actions. Both, being idealised theoretical systems of morality, inevitably fail to take account of certain aspects of our ordinary moral thinking. Kantian ethical theory has a tendency to advocate rigidly following what is thought to be one's duty for its own sake, whereas utilitarianism focusses on amounts of good and evil in the abstract as opposed to the people who will experience the pleasure or whatever. Taken to its extreme, the Kantian doctrine might entail, for example, that in a particular case it was morally right to keep a promise even if this resulted in many people suffering (because no account of the consequences or of general utility would be taken into account). Whereas utilitarianism might entail that it was right to kill an innocent person for the good of society (because individual liberty is not taken into account).

Insofar as Kantians and utilitarians have attempted to modify their views to account for such cases, they become less distinct, at least in practice, even though they may be unwilling to relinquish the basic emphasis of their outlook. To summarise, the Kantian system tends to emphasise the individual person and his or her rights and duties, particularly the principles of liberty and justice (as desert); utilitarianism stresses the notion of the public good, looking to the consequences of actions with respect to the principles of utility and justice (as equal treatment). So, when Downie and Telfer advocate a form of ideal rule utilitarianism which is also based on respect for persons (Downie and Telfer 1980), this may be quite realistic as a reflection of our ordinary moral thinking, although it may not be logically consistent as a system of morality in itself.

An 'ethic of care'

Kantian and utilitarian moralities are based on a system of individualised rights and duties, emphasising abstract moral principles, impartiality and rationality. Some commentators, particularly feminists, have termed this an 'ethic of justice'. They have argued that it is a very male-oriented system of morality which does not take account of approaches to ethics which tend to be adopted by women and which emphasise responsibility rather than duty and relationships rather than principles – an 'ethic of care' (Gilligan 1982). Others have argued that it is dangerous and incorrect to attribute what has been termed an 'ethic of care' simply to women (Farley 1993; Tronto 1993). Research has shown that Afro-Americans, for example, adopt a view of the self which stresses a sense of cooperation, interdependence and collective responsibility, as opposed to the ethic of justice (Tronto 1993, p. 84). Tronto argues that an ethic of justice represents the dominant mode of moral thinking which reflects the power structure in society and tends to marginalise and exclude the experience of women, Black people, working class and other oppressed groups. The distinction between an ethic of care and an ethic of justice is summarised in Table 2.2 which is based on material from Farley (1993).

It may seem surprising, given social work's caring role, that little work has been done so far to examine the relevance of an

Table 2.2 *Ethics of justice and care*

	Justice	Care
key value	justice – reinforces separation of persons	care – represents connectedness
appeal to	principles	relationships
focus on	social contracts ranked order of values duty individual freedom	cooperation communication caring relationship between persons

ethic of care to professional practice. It can be linked to 'virtue-based' ethical theories (Aristotle 1954; MacIntyre 1982) which regard relationships with others as part of a person's identity, and being moral as being a certain kind of person. A virtue is a character trait which contributes towards some ideal of the good life, both for individuals and the society to which they belong. According to Poole (1991, p. 59):

> individuals will perform the required activities, not just because they think that they will contribute eventually to some end they believe in (though they will think that too), but because performing them is a way of expressing their identity, and is thus a component of their own well-being as individuals.

However, as Poole continues:

> This kind of identity is not available in the modern public sphere, and for that reason an ethic of virtue is not available either. The contrasting private realm does, however, provide identities of this kind. Being a mother is, for example, assumed to involve a set of responsibilities to others which are both necessary to sustain the family and also a mode of individual fulfilment (ibid.).

To argue for the inclusion of an ethic of care or virtue-based ethics would entail challenging the separation of the public and private domains and reframing our conception of morality. This would mean challenging the dominant modes of thinking in our society which are also reflected in social work.

We will now look briefly at how some of these philosphical theories and concepts relate to recent developments in social work, including the challenges to traditional thinking posed by radical and anti-oppressive approaches.

Focus on the individual user as a person: 1960s and 1970s

In the 1960s and 1970s the literature on social work values tended to focus on issues related to the rights and interests of the individual user. The emphasis was very much on the *nature of the relationship* between the social worker and user, and in particular on how the social worker should treat the user. The kinds of principles articulated were about respecting the user as a person who had a right to make her/his own choices; not judging the user; accepting the user for what she/he is; and respecting confidentiality of information given to the social worker by the user (Biestek 1961; CCETSW 1976; Butrym 1976). At the heart of this set of values were the notions of *individualism* and *freedom*. Both these notions are, of course, at the core of prevailing ideology of western capitalist societies, and hence it is not surprising to find them predominant in the social work literature. What is surprising is the fact that so much of the literature on values in social work gave so much emphasis to the one-to-one social worker–user relationship, in abstraction from the agency and societal context in which it took place. Agency and societal considerations (for example, agency demands for confidential information, societal requirements for the control of 'deviants') were seen as constraints or limitations on the key principles of respecting the individual user's rights to choice and privacy.

Growing awareness of structural oppression: 1970s and 1980s

During the 1970s there was a growing awareness amongst social workers that treating each user as an individual, and seeing the problems faced by that user (such as poverty, homelessness, mental illness) as personal problems was, in effect, 'blaming the victims' for the structural inequalities in society. A range of literature was published advocating 'radical social work', which acknowledged social workers' role as agents of social control on behalf of an oppressive state, and called on them to raise the consciousness of the people they worked with, to encourage collective action for social change and build alliances with working class and trade union organisations (Bailey and Brake 1975; Brake and Bailey 1980; Corrigan and Leonard 1978). This literature of the 1970s did not discuss issues of ethics and values per se. This was probably partly because a lot of this thinking was based on Marxist perspectives. Marx himself discussed morality as a 'bourgeois illusion' – part of the prevailing ideology promoted by the ruling classes to control and dominate (Marx and Engels 1969; Lukes 1987). Secondly, a key theme of radical social work (although not always expressed very clearly) is 'praxis' – the notion of 'committed action'. On this view it makes no sense to regard values, theory and practice as separate. These ideas will be expanded upon in the next chapter.

Although the radical social work literature of the 1970s and early 1980s did not itself seem to influence the literature on social work values and ethics of the same period, the broadening of the understanding of oppression created by the feminist and anti-racist movements of the 1980s has now found its way into the lists of social work values. While the contributions from feminist and anti-racist theorists are often highly critical of the Marxist inspired radical social work (Dominelli and McLeod 1989; Day 1992; Ahmad 1990; Shah 1989; Dominelli 1988), they can nevertheless be seen to have grown out of, and alongside, the radical social work movement of the 1970s, and the collections of articles on radical work in the 80s have included substantial contributions from feminist and Black perspectives (Brake and Bailey 1980; Langan and Lee 1989). A concern for anti-oppressive practice is reflected in the list of values produced by the Council for Education and Training in Social Work (CCETSW 1989), an extract of which is shown in Table 2.3.

Jordan (1991) points out the contradictions between the traditional or Kantian values contained in the first part of the list (which includes variations on respect for persons, user self-determination and confidentiality) and the statements about structural oppression in the second part of the list. The individual freedom which social workers have a commitment to promote is, he claims, dependent on the structural inequalities in society which they also have a duty to challenge. He argues that the liberal values on which the first set of principles is based (including property rights and traditional personal morality based on notions of freedom of choice) are amongst the strongest intellectual defences of the privileges of wealth, whiteness, and

Table 2.3   *The values of social work*

---

1. Qualifying social workers should have a commitment to:
    - the value and dignity of individuals;
    - the right to respect, privacy and confidentiality;
    - the right of individuals and families to choose;
    - the strengths and skills embodied in local communities;
    - the right to protection of those at risk of abuse and exploitation and violence to themselves and others.
2. Qualifying social workers must be able to:
    - develop an awareness of the inter-relationship of the processes of structural oppression, race, class and gender;
    - understand and counteract the impact of stigma and discrimination on grounds of poverty, age, disability and sectarianism;
    - demonstrate an awareness of both individual and institutional racism and ways to combat both through anti-racist practice;
    - develop an understanding of gender issues and demonstrate anti-sexism in social work practice;
    - recognise the need for and seek to promote policies and practices which are non-discriminatory and anti-oppressive.

Source: CCETSW Paper 30, 'Requirements and Regulations for the Diploma in Social Work' (1989).

maleness upon which structural oppression is based (Jordan 1991, p. 8). This reasserts the point that social workers in the radical tradition had been making earlier; that the agenda of structural change conflicts with the individualist premises upon which social work is based.

While the respect for persons doctrine would entail that a user who was Black, for example, should be treated as an individual with rights, choices and desires, with no pre-judgements or prejudice based on irrelevant factors like skin colour, it would, in effect, be a 'colour-blind' approach. For being Black would be regarded as irrelevant, whereas the position adopted by anti-racist social workers would be to regard being Black as relevant, to see the user as a member of an oppressed group and to take this into account in the social work relationship. It is in the former colour-blind sense that many institutions, agencies and individuals may adopt and implement equal opportunities policies and claim to be 'non-racist'. The brief statements saying everyone will be treated equally 'irrespective of race, gender, religion, etc.' are good examples of this in that they do not recognise institutional or structural discrimination and therefore do not recognise the need for positive action to promote change.

The profession of social work in Britain, on paper at least, has moved beyond the colour-blind approach, and most literature and policy statements recognise institutional discrimination and express a commitment to challenge it. They recognise, for example, that Black people are under-represented in senior and professional posts, that social services departments are not meeting many of the needs of Black users, and that action needs to be taken to redress this imbalance. An essentially reformist position can be adopted which seeks to make changes to the law, to policies and their implementation to improve the situation. This would entail focussing not just on the individual, but the individual's position in society and working towards greater fairness and procedural justice in the distribution of rewards and punishments – basically a utilitarian outlook. However, the recognition and challenging of structural oppression – the recognition that the very rules and structures within which society operates reflect basic inequalities in power and that therefore fundamental and revolutionary change is required – is at odds with the emphasis on individual freedom of both Kantianism and utilitarianism; it calls for a more radical analysis and approach. Figure 2.1 summarises the differences between what I have called the Kantian, utilitarian and radical frameworks of moral thinking. It is a modified version of a diagram published previously (Banks 1990). The 'radical' category is very broad, and could include Marxist and anti-oppressive approaches, with the potential for further developments of an 'ethic of care'.

The influence of the ideologies of the new right: 1980s and 1990s

Simultaneously with the growing concern with structural oppression in the 1980s, has been the growing influence of the

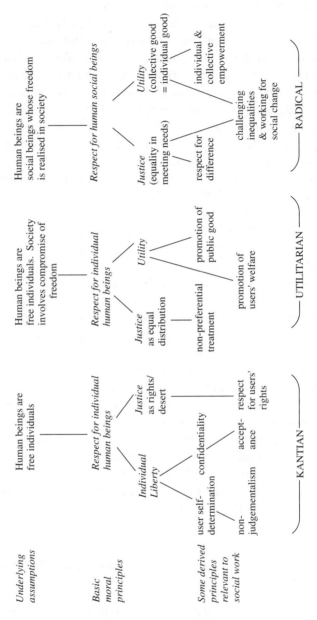

Figure 2.1 *Kantian, utilitarian and radical frameworks of moral thinking*

ideologies of the new right in legislation and policies relating to the public sector. This has been reflected in the growth in contracting out of services to the private sector; reduction in the power of professional groups and of the role of the welfare state; an emphasis on individuals' right to choose as the consumers of services; and a focus on individuals' rights and responsibilities as citizens to complain, or to care for their children or relatives. This does not seem to have changed the value statements of the profession. Perhaps this is not surprising since we have already noted that the value statements have tended to be somewhat divorced from the reality of social work practice. A more important reason is that aspects of the new right ideology appear superficially congruent with the key principles of the profession. Individuals' rights to choose and to complain could be seen to be part of the notion of respect for persons. The rights of users to information about their case, to be able to see their social work files, to know their rights to services and how to complain if they are not satisfied all fit in with the principle of treating users as rational, self-determining agents and can serve to protect them against the exercise of excessive parentalism or illegitimate power by social workers or social work agencies.

However, the focus of the new right ideology is not on the user as a whole person, but just one narrow part of being a person: namely in the role of 'consumer'. 'Consumer rights' are not the same as 'users' rights to self-determination', for the former are limited to the person in the role of a consumer of services, and the rights are to a certain pre-defined standard of service, a certain type of treatment, and a certain standard of goods. What is meant, in theory at least, by users' rights to self-determination relates to users as whole people – their rights to make choices, take decisions, to develop potential in a much broader sense than that of consumer.

Calling the user a consumer also serves to hide the fact of social worker as controller. It implies an active role and the possibility to exercise choice. It covers up the role of welfare as control – what some have called the 'new authoritarianism' which is based on the notion of the user as dangerous, as a risk to be assessed, as deviant and an outsider. This is another aspect of the policies and ideologies of the new right which is obviously contrary to the traditional social work values of respect for persons – the re-emergence of the Victorian distinction between the deserving and undeserving poor; the determination to punish and control those on the margins of society, the 'outcasts' or the 'underclass'. Some of these trends are reflected in the implementation of recent legislation relating to child protection and community care. While aspects of this legislation could be regarded as progressive in the promotion of children's rights and user participation in service delivery, other aspects are about treatment and control – the user as a problem to be technically assessed, clinically managed and processed through a proceduralised system. These policies and procedures are now based much more explicitly than in the past on the utilitarian values of procedural justice and the promotion of public welfare. They have generated not only procedures for assessment of risk and need, but also a host of codes of practice laying down users' rights, agency responsibilities and procedures for making complaints or for access to records, for example. In chapters 5 and 6 we will return to a discussion of the impact of these changes on the stated values of social work practice and the codes of ethics.

Ethical principles for social work in the 1990s

Our discussion of the social work literature on ethical principles suggests that there is not one commonly agreed and coherent set of principles for social work. However, by looking at the literature and at the actual practice of social work, I think it is possible to determine four basic or first order principles which are relevant to social work:

1. Respect for and promotion of individuals' rights to self-determination.
2. Promotion of welfare or well-being.
3. Equality.
4. Distributive justice.

None of these principles is straightforward in meaning or implications for practice.

1. **Self-determination** – we have already discussed the various meanings of 'self-determination' as:
   - *negative* – allowing someone to do as he or she chooses.
   - *positive* – creating the conditions which enable someone to become more self-determining.

   Recent emphasis on user participation (allowing users to have a say) and empowerment (developing users' skills and self-confidence so they can participate more) are manifestations of negative and positive self-determination. Self-determination in both senses has been for a long time one of the fundamental principles stated for social work practice, often phrased as 'client self-determination'. Yet while the social worker may sometimes be able to focus largely on one individual user and take on the role of advocate for the user's rights, often the social worker has to take into account the rights of significant others in a situation. In the interests of justice, it may not always be morally right to promote the user's rights at the expense of those of others.

2. **Welfare** – promoting someone's 'good' or welfare is also open to interpretation depending upon what our view is of what counts as human welfare, and whether we adopt our own view of what a person's welfare is, or the person's own conception of their welfare. It is dependent on cultural views about what are the basic human needs and what is a good quality of life. Much of modern social work is explicitly about ensuring that the best interests of particular user groups are served (for example, children in child protection work). Codes of ethics generally stress the social worker's duty to work in the user's interests. Often it is the social worker's view of what the user's interests are that is regarded as important. However, as with self-determination, whilst in some cases it may be clear-cut that it is the user's interests the social worker should be protecting, in other cases the social worker has to consider the interests of significant others and the 'public interest' (for example, through preventing re-

offending in work with young offenders). These various interests may conflict.

3. **Equality** – according to Spicker (1988, p. 125), equality means 'the removal of disadvantage'. This can be interpreted in many ways including:

   equal treatment – preventing disadvantage in access to services, including treatment without prejudice or favour. For example, it should not be the case that a middle-class white man seeking resources for his elderly mother is dealt with more quickly than a Black woman seeking similar support.

   equal opportunity – the removal of disadvantage in competition with others, giving people the means to achieve socially desired ends. For example, a social worker may arrange for an interpreter for a Bengali-speaking woman so that she can express her needs in detail and have the same opportunity as an English-speaking user to receive the services she requires.

   equality of result – in which disadvantages are removed altogether. For example, the residential home that would provide the best quality care for two older users with similar needs is very expensive. The user with a rich son who is prepared to pay is able to go to this home; the user who is poor is not. To achieve equality of result might entail the social services department paying the full fee for the poorer user, or, to avoid stigmatisation, the state providing free high quality care for all people with similar needs.

   Social workers are concerned to promote all three forms of equality, although equality of treatment is much easier to achieve than equality of oppportunity or result. Equality of treatment would follow logically from the principle of respect for persons. Equality of opportunity and of result require some more positive action to redress existing disadvantages, and may require additional resources or changes in government policy. To aim for equality of result may require structural changes in society – challenging certain people's existing rights to wealth, property and power. It is this type of principle that underpins some of the more radical and anti-oppressive approaches to social work.

4. **Distributive justice** – is about distributing goods according to certain rules and criteria. The criteria for distribution may vary from:
   - according to people's already existing rights (e.g., property rights).
   - according to desert.
   - according to need.

   Although justice and equality are linked, a concept of justice based on property rights or desert may result in inequality. Rawls' (1972) concept of justice, for example, is based on two principles: equality in the assignment of basic needs and resources; and social and economic inequalities only insofar as there are compensating benefits for everyone, especially the least advantaged. Although distributive justice per se is generally not listed amongst the social work principles, it is perhaps one of the most fundamental principles in the work (insofar as it is in the public sector) in that social workers are responsible for distributing public resources (whether they be counselling, care or money) according to certain criteria based variously on rights, desert and need. I would argue that this principle is in operation in much social work decision-making and is becoming more central in the present climate as resource allocation becomes a more common role for social workers.

Conclusions

In this chapter we have explored some of the philosophical foundations of the ethical principles underlying social work. We have argued that the stated principles of the profession are broadly 'Kantian' and rest on the doctrine of respecting the individual as a rational and self-determining human being. We suggested, however, that the traditional social work values tend to focus on the *content* of the social worker–user relationship. Whereas, for social work, the *context* in which it is practised, as part of a welfare bureaucracy with a social control and resource-rationing function (based on more utilitarian values), also places ethical duties upon the social worker which may conflict with her duties to the user as an individual. These conflicts can be seen to reflect the tensions and contradictions of the welfare state which were discussed in chapter 1.

A third 'radical' framework of moral thinking was identified – encompassing both Marxist and anti-oppressive approaches to practice. Its underlying assumptions which are based on a commitment to equality of result and a view of humans as essentially social (focussing on relationships, cooperation, collectivity), are fundamentally at odds with the Kantian-utilitarian framework of moral thinking which is firmly based in the Western liberal tradition of individual rights and duties.

Exercise 2

Aims of the exercise – to encourage the reader to reflect critically on the stated values of the profession in the light of his/her own value commitments.

1. List what you think are the important values *you* hold as a social worker.
2. How do they compare with the list produced by CCETSW in Table 2.3?
3. Can you suggest any modifications/additions to the CCETSW list?

3

Values and Knowledge

This chapter will explore the interrelationship between knowledge and values through discussing the value implications of some of the theories and models proposed for social work. It will highlight the tension between Kantian, utilitarian and radical values discussed in chapter 2.

Knowledge as value-laden

'How do we know the world?', 'what do we know?' 'what is the status of that knowledge?' are all questions that have long puzzled philosophers, so it is perhaps not surprising if they have also given social work theorists some food for thought. In considering knowledge for social work and its relationship to the values of the occupation, there are a number of concepts and ideas that need to be taken into account. Knowledge is sometimes divided into two kinds: knowing that and why (theoretical knowledge) and knowing how (practical knowledge). 'Knowing that' might be knowledge of 'facts' about the world, such as 'there is a user in the waiting room', which could be said to be known through experience and could be verified by going and looking in the waiting room. 'Knowing why' might be a more theoretical kind of knowledge, such as 'this user is hiding in the corner because she is suffering from phobic anxiety', which would be verified with reference to various generalisations in psychoanalytic theory. 'Knowing how' is about how to do things like 'writing a pre-sentence report', or 'assessing the needs of a person with disabilities'. Obviously in social work all these kinds of knowledge are important, although the practical knowledge is often described as 'skills' or 'techniques' rather than 'knowledge'.

It is often assumed that knowing that, or 'factual' knowledge, is value-free. To say we know that there is a user in the waiting room surely does not entail commitments to any particular value position? In one sense this is true. In another sense, if we consider more carefully we realise that just seeing the person in the waiting room as a 'user' is already constituting the situation in a particular way. We are already categorising the person in terms of our relationship to her, which may have connotations of the user as needing to be helped, or as part of the bureaucratic social work system which involves people sitting in waiting rooms in a subservient fashion. We have already evaluated the situation according to our own perspective. This is not the same as making a straightforward value statement like 'that user ought to be helped', but it does have value connotations. The second statement, which is based on more obviously theoretical knowledge about phobic anxiety, might more readily be regarded as having value overtones, as it rests on a theory about how humans think and act, which in turn is based on some fundamental presuppositions about the nature of human beings.

The situation is similar with knowing how, or practical knowledge. Skills such as writing pre-sentence reports or assessing users' needs already presuppose a lot of factual and theoretical knowledge about the nature of the legal system, or what criteria are to be used in the assessment, for example, which in turn is based on views about what is a need, or who ought to get help. These are fundamentally evaluative presuppositions. This is not to say that in order for a social worker to be able to do an assessment of a user's needs she has to know what concept of need the assessment is based upon, just that any assessment of need presupposes some concept of what need is, and this will be an evaluative concept. The doing of the assessment is not 'value-neutral', even if the social worker is simply filling in a form designed by someone else.

Further, it could be argued that the good or 'competent' social worker – the reflective practitioner (Schön 1987) – needs to be aware both of the societal or professional values underlying her work and of her own values, and should adopt a critical stance to her practice. Some commentators have argued that the social worker should not only be a reflective practitioner, but also a committed practitioner, working for change in society through her action (Ronnby 1992). This fusion of reflection and action has been called 'praxis' – a concept that can be found in Aristotle and is developed in Marxist thinking and through the works of Paulo Freire. This is moving beyond simply stating that values, knowledge and skill are inseparable, to a normative statement about what the role of the social worker ought to be. If the social worker compartmentalises reflection (values and knowledge) from action (use of skill), she is, in fact, deceiving herself. She is in 'bad faith', as Sartre would say, because she is pretending that her action can be value-free and purely 'technical'. She is denying her own responsibility as a moral agent for that action. For Freire, reflection without action results in 'mentalism', and action without reflection in 'activism'; and both are empty (Freire 1972).

So, we have argued that there is no such thing as value-free knowledge, and that values, knowledge and skills are inseparably related. Obviously there are degrees of value-ladenness, which is reflected in the fact that we do tend to talk as if knowledge and values are separate entities in our everyday discussions, and sometimes it can be useful to separate them analytically.

Theories, models and techniques in social work

In looking at the values underpinning social work knowledge, we will briefly explore some of the theories, models and techniques that have been developed for social work to consider what value assumptions underlie them. Before we do this, it will be helpful to clarify some of the terminology that will be used, as this can be confusing. Texts on social work knowledge tend to include discussion of a whole range of entities includ-ing ideologies, perspectives, approaches, theories, models, techniques and skills. Sometimes terms are used interchangeably, like ideology or perspective, theory or model, for example. In this book, the following definitions will be used:

- **Ideology** – a system of belief about the nature of human beings which is held by some group of people as giving rise to their way of life (Stevenson, 1974, p. 7).
- **Perspective** – a particular way of looking at the world. It may be from a particular ideological or theoretical viewpoint, or some other standpoint.
- **Theory** – strictly speaking a general rule or law which seeks to offer an explanation or understanding of some aspect of the world. Very often, however, the term is used to mean 'theoretical system' which is a coherent set of explanatory generalisations. It will be used in this way here.
- **Model** – a descriptive classification of part of the world; a model has less explanatory power than a theory.
- **Technique or skill** – the practical ability to do something.

There is often confusion in the social work literature about what is being talked about. Obviously all these concepts are inter-connected – models and techniques may form part of a theoretical system, which in turn may be based upon certain ideological beliefs about the nature of human society. The use of a term like 'perspective' or 'approach' avoids having to specify exactly what is being talked about – which can be useful, but also misleading. In social work it is useful because knowledge for social work tends to be 'eclectic' – that is, it is drawn from a range of theories and models from various academic disciplines and professions. In the gathering together and modification of these pieces of theories and models it is not always clear what they are being made into; to say they constitute an approach or a perspective is fairly all-encompassing and vague and is therefore an easy option. It also reflects the fact that research into social work practitioners' use of theory suggests that many rarely consciously use a particular identifiable theory, rather they use 'practice wisdom' based on an amalgam of learning from experience and bits of theories and techniques that have been read about or learnt on the job (Curnock and Hardicker 1979; Roberts 1990).

The social work knowledge base

Many people have thought it important that social work should have a distinct 'knowledge base'. This stems partly from the quest to establish social work as a profession, since one of the necessary features of a profession has been said to be that it is underpinned by a specialist body of knowledge. However, despite much discussion and many attempts to define a unique body of knowledge for social work, most commentators would tend to agree that these attempts have failed. There are, no doubt, many reasons why. The most significant is probably that the roles and tasks undertaken by social workers are so varied and the contexts so diverse that it has been difficult to agree a common aim or purpose for social work. Without this it seems almost impossible to develop a unifying body of knowledge. The kinds of statements about the purpose of social work which have emerged, such as 'assisting people in their problems of social functioning' (Butrym 1976, p. 13) have hardly been sufficiently specific to define a specialist area of knowledge. Knowledge in this context can be defined as the 'acquaintance with or theoretical or practical understanding of some branch of science, art, learning, or other area involving study, research or practice, and the acquisition of skills' (Morales and Sheafor 1986, p. 173). What has happened in social work is that theories from various other academic and professional disciplines have been imported and modified, and a plethora of models or approaches have been developed, alongside specialist techniques to apply to particular types of situation or problem. So, although it is true to say that it is possible to define a knowledge base for social work, it is not unified or distinctive.

It was suggested earlier that the kind of knowledge needed for social work includes both theoretical (knowing why and knowing that) and practical knowledge (knowing how). These might be broken down as follows:

Theoretical	1.	Sociological and psychological theories, e.g. Marxist theory, Freudian theory.
Theoretical	2.	'Middle range theories' or models, e.g. labelling theory, deviancy theory.

Practical   Methods and techniques, e.g. case manage-
                      ment, advocacy.

Although there have been attempts to develop all-embracing
theories which can cover the whole of social work practice and
include many of the divergent sets of theories, models and
techniques, these have been heavily criticised as being so all-
inclusive as to fail in their purpose of integrating or unifying the
practice of social work (Howe 1987; Roberts 1990). We have
already suggested that many practitioners do not see themselves
as consciously using theory, but rather relying on 'practice
wisdom' or an eclectic collection of useful bits of theory drawn
from different places interwoven with their own learning from
practice experience. Some have called this 'practice theory'
(Curnock and Hardicker 1979) and distinquished it from
'theories of practice', which would be the sociological or
psychological theories mentioned above. Others have disdained
to call this eclecticism 'theory' and regarded as a dangerous
practice the magpie approach of the taking of useful parts of
many different theories, which out of context may be
misunderstood or inappropriate, contradictory or out of tune with
the basic values of social work (Payne 1991, pp. 47–50).

   This is why it is important to consider values in relation to the
knowledge base of social work. For there has been a tendency in
the social work literature to separate knowledge and values. The
texts that cover various theoretical approaches to social work
tend to look at the explanatory theories and models, the aims and
methods of each approach, but rarely explicitly look at the
underlying values (e.g. Howe 1987; Payne 1991). One text on
social work models, which does explicitly cover values, includes
this in a separate section and does not relate the values of social
work to the section on models (Butrym 1976).

Theories and perspectives for social work practice

There are many texts which list and compare different theories
and models, all identifying slightly different configurations (e.g.

Butrym 1976; Howe 1987; Payne 1991). One of the problems is that they tend to include a whole range of theories, models and techniques, some of which are more comprehensive, and therefore more value-laden, than others. Payne (1991, pp. 236–7) makes a useful distinction between:

- **comprehensive theories** offering a system of thought to cover all the practice that social workers might want to undertake in casework, residential and group work, such as psychodynamic, behavioural or systems theories.
- **application theories** offering useful broad ideas which are widely applicable and some specific techniques designed to apply to particular problems or situations, such as crisis intervention, task-centred or empowerment and advocacy.
- **specific theories** offering ideas and techniques which would benefit social workers in their work whichever theory they were using, such as communication theory.
- **perspective theories** offering a way of looking at the world, particularly personal and social change, attached to which are a number of ideas about practice, such as radical, humanist or existentialist theories.

I would argue that it is only possible to identify value assumptions in comprehensive and perspective theories. This is not to say that advocates of application or specific theories do not do so from an explicit or implicit value position; just that a particular value position is not inherent in the theory itself, and will depend upon the broader theoretical or ideological perspective adopted. For example, an empowerment approach could be advocated by a radical Marxist, or feminist, as part of the route towards revolutionary change. The key value position might be a belief in equality of result, viewing empowerment as a collective taking of power by members of an oppressed group. A reformist might use it to work towards changing policies and laws, based on a principle of distributive justice entailing power sharing between service users and officials. A conservative might adopt a citizens' rights approach to empowerment with the aim of giving individuals more power and reducing the role of the welfare state. The key underpinning principle might be individual self-determination, giving users the right to complain if certain standards of service are not met.

Using Payne's (1991) categorisation and account of social work theories, we will now examine the value implications of the ones he describes as comprehensive and perspective theories, which are:

psychodynamic
behavioural   COMPREHENSIVE
systems/ecological
cognitive

radical   PERSPECTIVE
humanist/existential

In assessing the extent to which the stated values of social work are reflected in these theories, it is important to remember that a basic assumption of both Kantian and utilitarian theories is that human beings are viewed as individuals who are free to make decisions and choices. These assumptions of individuality and freedom can be regarded as the fundamental basis of western, liberal conceptions of morality. Freedom (as the opposite of determinism) is certainly presupposed in our whole way of thinking and speaking about morality, which assumes people are capable of making choices and are responsible for their behaviour, which it is therefore appropriate to praise or blame. While it may be acknowledged that on some occasions people are not capable of making choices (their mental capacities may be permanently or temporarily impaired, for example) and sometimes people's behaviour may be regarded as determined by forces outside their control, these are regarded as exceptions. If determinism was the norm – that is, if people's decisions and choices were predictable on the basis of knowledge about physical, psychological or social causation – then it would make no sense to praise or blame people for their actions.

Psychodynamic theories

There is no doubt that psychoanalytic theories derived from Freud have been very influential in social work. However, social work has not adopted psychoanalytic theory, or its associated therapeutic techniques, per se. Various theories, models and approaches have been developed for social work which are derivative of psychoanalytic theory. According to Payne (1991, p. 75), there are two important ideas underpinning the theory which are:

> *psychic determinism* – the principle that actions or behaviour arise from people's thought processes rather than just happen;
> *the unconscious* – the idea that some thinking and mental activity is hidden from our knowledge.

Although different variations of psychodynamic theory for social work have different emphases (such as problem-solving, pyscho-social functioning, or ego psychology), it could be argued that they all rest to some degree on the principle of pyschic determinism, they focus on the individual, and tend to adopt a scientific approach which puts the social worker in the role of expert, using a medical model which uses language like 'diagnosis' and 'treatment'. This is not to say that the user is not seen as the main agent of change, since the ways in which psychoanalytic theories have been adapted for social work tend to take account of the important values of social work, including user self-determination, and incorporate a social dimension. Nevertheless, their roots in psychoanalytic theory mean that the primary focus for the explanation of people's behaviour is deterministic. This kind of view is in conflict with the principle of respect for persons as rational, self-determining human beings with the ability to make free choices.

Behaviourist theories

Again, theories from another discipline, behavioural psychology, have been adapted for use in social work. In contrast to psychodynamic theory, behavioural social work concentrates on observable behaviour and uses learning theories to analyse and modify behaviour. Unlike psychodynamic theory, there is a focus on the present rather than the past, and on the external and observable, rather than the internal and reported. It also sees itself as scientific, based on principles 'derived from empirical research about how behaviour is learned, maintained and unlearned' (Hudson and Macdonald 1986, p. 2) with a focus on changing the individual. It is also a deterministic theory, although this time it is a materialistic determinism, rather than pyschological. Behavioural theories have been sharply criticised in social work for being excessively mechanistic and even for being unethical, in that some of the techniques they use (such as token-economy or aversion therapy) are incompatible with respecting individuals as human beings with free will and dignity (Butrym 1976, p. 30). They also tend to focus on the ends (the change to be brought about) at the expense of the means (the methods used). This can be, and has been, counteracted, and as with pyschodynamic theory many versions of behavioural social work have been modified and adapted to take into account such issues. The important point to note is that the fundamental view of human nature on which behavioural approaches are primarily based is deterministic.

Cognitive theories

Although such theories are not yet well-developed in social work, and are ultimately a derivation of behaviourism, Payne (1991) argues that they do form a separate category. They are concerned with people's thinking and assume people's behaviour is directed by thoughts rather than unconscious drives, conflicts and feelings. They tend to use explanations which rely on rational control of people's behaviour. Payne suggests that cognitive approaches did not make a significant impact on social work until humanistic elements were added which permitted the user's perceptions of the world to be regarded as accurate (that is, they allowed for a more subjectivist approach). Goldstein (1981) emphasises the need for a moral code/social philosophy, including regarding people as searching for and moving towards their own goals and constructing their own versions of reality through what they have learnt. This seems more in tune with the value of respect for persons as rational and self-determining beings. According to Payne:

> Overall, we can see cognitive approaches as offering a useful way of understanding social work in a way that emphasises clients' rational capacity to manage their lives, and enhances that capacity with clear and well-tried techniques. Allied with humanist views of the process and related values which respect and involve clients, cognitive approaches to social work retain many of social works's basic caring values within a framework of effective action, They are, as yet, relatively untried in everyday social work practice (Payne 1991, p. 200).

Systems theories

Payne categorises systems theories along with ecological theories which emphasise the adaptiveness of people to their environments. Systems approaches in social work have their origins in von Bertalanffy's (1971) biological theory which states that all organisms are systems, composed of sub-systems, and are in turn part of super-systems. This can be applied to social systems like families and societies. There have been several variations of systems theory developed for social work, one of the most well-known of which is that of Pincus and Minahan (1973). They argue that people depend on systems in their immediate social environment for a satisfactory life, so social work must focus on the interventions and linkages between people and social systems. They distinguish the 'client system' (the people who engage in working with the social work or 'change agent' system) from the 'target system' (the people whom the change agent is trying to change to achieve its aims). As Payne comments, such theories are among the few comprehensive sociologically based theories of social work, very different from the traditional focus on individualisation and psychology. However, systems theories have been criticised as being over-inclusive (Butrym 1976; Payne 1991; Roberts 1990); they cannot explain why things happen, they just offer ways of seeing what is happening. The technical terminology of 'change agents' and 'target systems' does not fit in easily with the traditional social work values, and the emphasis on technological strategies for change again tends to put the social worker in the role of expert and emphasises the ends to be achieved (the change). It is difficult to reconcile the value of respect for users as persons, with the 'client as system'.

Radical perpectives

'Radical' approaches to social work have been influenced by Marxism and shift the focus of the work away from the individual and on to the structures of society. We have already discussed the development of Marxist-inspired radical social work in the 1970s, and noted how this paved the way for the anti-oppressive approaches of the 1980s (see chapter 2). While there is a variety of radical approaches, what they have in common is a critique of traditional social work theories and methods as tending to focus on changing individuals rather than changing the social structures that cause problems like poverty, poor housing, patriarchy or racism (Corrigan and Leonard 1978; Brake and Bailey 1980; Langan and Lee 1989). Feminist, anti-racist and other anti-oppressive approaches which focus on the structural causes of social problems would tend to fall into this category – although it should be noted that not all 'feminist' or 'anti-racist' approaches are radical; some may be liberal or reformist. Although radical social work would want to hold on to the idea of respecting the user as a person, the view of 'person' is not that of a free individual in the Kantian sense. It is more a vision of a 'social being' – which leads to a recommendation for social work practice which involves raising the consciousness of individuals to recognise the nature of their oppression and developing their capacities to work collectively for social change. Traditional morality (linked to the Kantian notion of individuals following their duty for its own sake) would be regarded as a system of rules and principles reflecting the interests and values of powerful and dominant groups in society. Such perspectives, therefore, would reject the traditional social work values insofar as these focus on promoting the freedom of the individual, but would include a commitment to positive freedom – that is, the social worker should work towards creating the conditions under which users can exercise more choice and develop their potential as human beings in a socialist/non-oppressive society.

From the point of view of traditional social work, radical approaches have been criticised for focussing less on the here and now, the immediate and pressing problems facing individuals, and more on the creation of a better society in the future. This might involve treating individual users as a means to an end, and not respecting their own current expressions of needs and wants. In the short term, Marxist approaches could be interpreted as recommending a utilitarian approach – using people as a means to an end, for the greater good of humanity as a whole. Yet, as with all the other perspectives and theories described above, there are many versions of 'radical' social work which have different emphases. Many feminist and anti-racist approaches are concerned with individual empowerment and working for small 'prefigurative' changes within their own agencies, rather than massive structural changes in society (Langan and Lee 1989, p. 14).

Humanist/existential perspectives

Payne groups together a number of models of social work practice which have in common ideas that:

> human beings are trying to make sense of the world that they experience, that social workers are trying to help people gain the

skills to explore themselves and the personal meaning that they attach to the world they perceive and which affects them, and that their interpretations of their own selves are valid and worthwhile (Payne 1991, p. 169).

One of the strongest influences on the development of 'humanist' ideas in social work is the work of Carl Rogers (1951; 1961) in the field of counselling, where he focusses on the importance of the relationship between the counsellor and user and stresses that the approach should be non-directive, non-judgemental, empathic and that the counsellor/worker should have 'unconditional positive regard' for the user. There is a focus on the uniqueness of each individual and the importance of the self seeking personal growth. There are many variations on these themes, including the work of Brandon (1976) who develops an approach based on Zen philosophy, England (1986) who develops the idea of social ·work as 'art', and Wilkes (1981) who advocates a strongly Kantian approach to the rights of users to freedom from social work interference and speaks of the user as 'a mystery to be apprehended'. Butrym groups such approaches under the heading of 'ministration in love' and sees their foundations as largely derived from the Judeo-Christian tradition and the existentialism of philosophers such as Buber and Kierkegaard (Butrym 1976, p. 26). Howe (1987) categorises them as 'client-centred approaches', all of which are based on the view that people are subjects to be understood in terms of the meanings they attach to their own lives, and not objects to be explained, controlled, acted upon or changed according to external mechanistic or scientific laws. Such a humanistic perspective is entirely congruent with the stated values of social work founded on the principle of respect for persons. It seems strange, therefore, that such approaches are not more widespread, and that comprehensive theories with associated methods and techniques have not been more widely developed and accepted in social work. Payne (1991) suggests that the location of social work in bureaucratic agencies with social control functions is not conducive to the approach of humanist therapies where users are in control of the exploration and the worker has a non-directive role.

Incompatible values?

This brief discussion of some of the theories and perspectives that have been promoted for social work practice suggests that the values underlying the majority of the theories do not appear compatible with stated values of social work. Most of the theories and approaches – particularly the most dominant one in social work, psychodynamic theory – are based on determinist assumptions about human thought and action and have a tendency to adopt a 'scientific' approach, which entails regarding the user as an object to be changed rather than a person to be respected. The theories or perspectives which are closest to the traditional social work values – the humanist, and to some extent possibly the cognitive – are both under-developed as comprehensive theories for social work practice. It is easy to explain why this might be the case, as suggested above, because the conditions within which social work is actually practised do not lend themselves to the use of approaches and techniques based on humanist values or assumptions about users as rational agents. Users are usually people who are in difficulty, facing crisis, in need of help and therefore less capable of rational decision-making than they or others might be in different circumstances. Social workers are often acting within the constraints of the law, agency policy, limited time and resources, and bureaucratic procedures which are more conducive to treating the user as a 'case' than as a person. A concern to establish social work as a profession based on a sound and 'scientific' knowledge base also encourages the use of approaches and techniques that have their origins in positivistic conceptions of natural science (technical and objective) rather than humanistic views of social science (intentional and subjective). The idea of social work as an 'art' may not appeal to a profession trying to establish itself and gain respect amongst the doctors and lawyers, and looking for specific techniques which will work, the results of which can be measured. What is puzzling is less why the theories for social work do not reflect the stated values of the profession, but more why the stated values are not in tune with the actual theories and day-to-day practice?

There are a number of explanations for the persistence of the 'respect for persons' approach in the stated values of social work. First, the separation of knowledge and values in the literature and much of social work education has discouraged discussion and analysis of their inter-relationships. Secondly, it may be precisely because of the contexts in which social workers work and the predominance of technicist values in these institutions that it is important that the profession holds on to an alternative vision of the human being as a free agent to be respected. Since users are usually powerless, lacking real options for choice and needing to be dealt with quickly, it is tempting to treat all users in a mechanistic way. The doctrine of respect for persons is a reminder of another way of looking at people and treating them. Perhaps the two ways of looking at users (or human beings in general) are not as incompatible as we might have thought. They may be contradictory, in that it is difficult to see a user as both free and determined simultaneously, but perhaps they are compatible in that they are two ways of looking at the world, both of which are valid.

Strawson (1959) has argued that the language of determinism is compatible with the language of free will insofar as they may be regarded as complementary attitudes towards particular actions. The reactive attitude characterises the interpersonal behaviour of 'normal' adults, assuming free, purposive behaviour (free will); while the objective attitude is applied in cases where reactive attitudes are suspended. An objective attitude might be applied to a particular person because of illness, insanity, or when she wants to escape the strain of involvement (Downie and Telfer 1969, p. 108). This kind of view is developed further by Hollis, who suggests that purposive explanation of behaviour is primary and is generally used until this type of explanation breaks down; and what is left, the incompletely explained part of a person's behaviour, is explained causally (Hollis 1977).

This would suggest that there is no incompatibility in social workers regarding some people as incapable of rational, self-determined action and as needing treatment, while at the same time respecting others as rational, self-determining agents. The problem with behaviourist or psychoanalytic theories is that they focus excessively on the objective causal mode of explanation. However, we would be looking for a theory which took acount of the contradictions – the fact that all human beings, including users of social work services, are both free and unfree, both objects and subjects, and action can be explained both in terms of external causes and internal reasons or purposes. Determinism could be regarded as a framework of social norms and rules of behaviour (including morality) and of modes of explanation and thought (including scientific thought) which sets limits to people's action and thinking, outside of which it is very difficult to think or act. Within this framework human beings do have choices and do act according to their own purposes and desires. What is important about this framework, however, is that it is a *social* framework, and society is made up not of unique individuals, but of social beings who relate to each other in the context of publicly understood rules and norms. If we hold this kind of view, however, it does become very difficult to sustain the first basic premise of traditional morality – that of individualism, which sees the individual as the primary mode of being. The notion of an individual person only makes sense in the context of a world of other people; the individual has no identity in her or himself, except in relation to others. That is, I can have no concept of myself as a separate being without defining myself as not other people. Or, as Sartre puts it, 'I need the other in order to realise fully all the structures of my being' (Sartre 1969, p. 222).

Generally, much of the social work literature on ethics and values states the social context of people's behaviour. Indeed, social work is claimed to be concerned with social functioning (the interaction between people and their environment). However, the distinctness of individuals from their social context is nevertheless maintained; and the emphasis is still on the abstract individual as the primary unit of being, to whom certain rights attach to protect her/him from outside intrusions. This is why the Kantian-utilitarian liberal morality has been criticised as 'alienated' morality, for the social and moral laws come from outside the person, rather than being regarded as an internal part of her or his very being.

Wittgenstein's ideas about understanding people's actions within a public context of rule-governed behaviour (Wittgenstein 1967) have been applied in the social sciences by Winch (1958) and have been expounded in social work literature, particularly by Ragg (1977). On this type of view, to understand a rule is to know how to act in certain situations and to be able to give reasons for action, which presupposes a public, social context. On this interpretation of human beings as rational in a social context, the principle of respect for persons would become respect for social beings (rather than individuals). This is close to Marx's idea of the dignity of people as social beings whose natures are fully realised in a truly collective society: 'man [*sic*] is not an abstract being squatting outside the world. He is the human world, the state, the society' (Marx 1963, p. 43).

At a theoretical level there is a need to go beyond the dualisms of the individual and society, free will and determinism, means and ends, knowledge and values, and to adopt a more holistic approach. At the level of practice this means acknowledging that the context within which social work takes place is based on values which are about public welfare, social control, and encouraging the individual to fit into society, and that the kinds of theories that tend to fit this role are deterministic and mechanistic; but within this framework, at the micro-level of the one-to-one relationship with the user, if we can 'bracket off' the societal and agency constraints, we can try to treat the user as a person to be respected. 'Bracketting off' should not mean pretending that the context of constraints and utilitarian values does not exist. That would be self-deception. The social worker must acknowledge that she is in the role of social worker, a publicly paid helper or controller, and the laws of the land and the rules of the agency form part of that relationship with the user. That is not to say that the social worker cannot or should not relate to users as a fellow human being – feel for users' pains, empathise with their suffering – but that both the user and

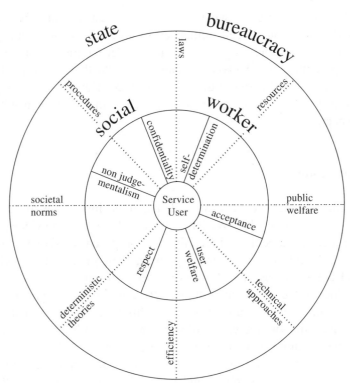

Figure 3.1   *The constraints on the social worker–user relationship*

the worker must be aware that the relationship is governed by additional and different rules to a purely personal relationship. Figure 3.1 illustrates this situation.

For example, a social worker making an assessment of the needs of a person with a disability is doing so within a framework prescribed by her agency – probably using a standard form, and only able to offer a certain level of resources to this user. Yet within this framework the user can be spoken to and treated with respect and honesty. Similarly, a decision may have been made by a case conference that a child should be removed from her parents because the parents are not capable of giving adequate care. This may have been the outcome of a utilitarian process of moral decision-making involving the weighing up of risks and working out what would be the best outcome for the child. It may have been influenced by pyschodynamic theories about families and the causes of abuse. Yet within this process the parents may be given a chance to state their views, told honestly what the role of the Social Services Department is, and given the opportunity to get legal advice – that is, treated with respect.

Conclusions

In this chapter we have argued that it is impossible to have value-free knowledge. We have suggested that the knowledge – the theories, models and techniques – proposed for social work in the literature tends to presuppose a view of human thought and behaviour as causally determined – by unconscious psychological factors, by natural instincts, the social environment or by social and economic structures. This view of human nature fits uneasily with the values of social work as traditionally stated in the literature, which are based on the notion of the user as a person who is free to make choices and to determine her or his action according purposes and goals. We suggest that both the theories for social work and the values of social work need to be modified and interconnected. The predominant theories tend to lay too much stress on scientific and technical approaches and to objectify the user, whereas the values focus on the individual in the abstract and assume freedom and choice which plays down societal and agency constraints. The reflective practitioner needs to be aware of these tensions and contradictions, in order to understand her role in relation to users and to realise that she is both a publicly paid professional with some 'expert' knowledge whose aim is to change and control behaviour, and a fellow human being whose aim is to relate to and empathise with the user. Neither role is 'pure', and the praxis of social work, that is the unity of practice-informed-by-and-informing-theory-and-values, reflects this.

4

Professional Codes of Ethics

This chapter looks at the meaning of 'professionalism' and the role of professional codes of ethics in social work. The discussion is illustrated through examination of codes of ethics from 15 different countries.

Professionalism and codes of ethics

In most western countries the occupation of social work has a code of ethics. This is often said to be one of the defining features of a profession. In the 1960s and 1970s there was much debate about whether social work was a profession (Etzioni 1969; Toren 1972). The 'trait' theory of professionalism tended to be used, which maintained that, to be a profession, an occupation must possess certain characteristics. One of the most commonly quoted lists of ideal attributes of a profession is that of Greenwood (1957) which includes the following:

1. a basis of systematic theory
2. authority recognised by the clientele of the professional group
3. broader community sanction and approval of this authority
4. a code of ethics regulating relationships of professionals with users and colleagues
5. a professional culture sustained by formal professional associations.

Additional features listed as important by other commentators include: the service is for the public good; there is a requirement for training and education; there is a need to demonstrate competence by passing a test (a qualification) (Millerson 1964, p. 4). Social work has often been defined as a 'semi-profession' because while it meets some of these criteria, it does not meet them all fully. First, as was suggested in chapter 3, it does not rest on a firm theoretical knowledge base. Secondly, members cannot claim a monopoly of exclusive skills – many people not qualified as social workers may be performing the same or comparable tasks. Thirdly, in Britain, unlike most other European countries, the title of 'social worker' is not protected by law and unqualified people or volunteers may be called 'social workers'. Fourthly, as was suggested in chapter 1, there is a public ambivalence regarding the authority of social workers. Finally, social workers' special area of competence (their function) is less well-defined compared with the so-called 'fully fledged' professions, and their period of training is relatively short (Toren 1972, p. 52).

Recent commentators have criticised the 'trait theory', suggesting that it is simply taking as a model the old-established professions, such as medicine and the law, and defining any occupation that does not share the same characteristics as less than a profession (Wilding 1982; Abbott and Wallace 1990; Hugman 1991). Commentators have pointed out how the 'caring professions' such as social work, nursing, and occupational therapy have tended traditionally to be women's occupations and have been denied full professional status partly for this reason. Caring work (meaning caring for others) is thought to be women's work; it has less status and prestige and does not require special knowledge and skills. Medicine is not a 'caring profession' in the same way; although the profession includes the 'service ideal', this is the idea of commitment to serve patients – caring *about* them not *for* them. It is the nurses who care for patients in performing the everyday tasks of bathing, or feeding (Hugman 1991, p. 17).

While 'caring professionals' may not be regarded as full professionals in many people's eyes, and are given less status and recognition than, for example, doctors, they do wield considerable power, particularly over users. And this aspect of professionalism – the claim to expert knowledge, the control not just of resources, but also the power to define the terms of the professional–user relationship – has been strongly attacked from many quarters, ranging from right to left. Illich speaks of the 'disabling professions' arguing that power and control over individuals' lives has been taken away by so-called 'experts' such as doctors, teachers or social workers (Illich 1977). Professions can be seen as protective and exclusive groups, seeking to retain power over their own occupations and hence over users. These criticisms can be levelled at social work, regardless of whether one regards it as an aspirant profession, a semi-profession or a profession.

What is a code of ethics?

It is partly an acknowledgement of this power that professionals have – particularly related to their possession of specialist knowledge and skills, which may not be fully (or even partially) understood by the users – that professions are said to need codes of ethics. The British Association of Social Workers (BASW) code states:

> Social work is a professional activity. Implicit in its practice are ethical principles which prescribe the professional responsibility of the social worker. The primary objective of the code of ethics is to make these implicit principles explicit *for the protection of clients* [my emphasis] (BASW 1988).

The term 'code of ethics' is used to cover quite a broad range of different types of codes of conduct or behaviour. Millerson sees professional ethics as a part of what is entailed by 'professional conduct'. He divides professional conduct into professional practice and professional ethics. This is quite a useful distinction which links to a distinction that will be developed later between codes of practice and codes of ethics. Thus, according to Millerson (1964, p. 149), professional conduct consists of:

1. *Professional practice* which relates to the adoption of schedules of uniform professional fees and charges, standard forms of contract, regulation of competition for projects;
2. *Professional ethics* which are concerned with moral directives guiding the relationship between the professional and others; they are designed to distinguish right from wrong action. A professional ethic may be a formal code, or an informal understanding.

It is the latter, written codes of ethics, which concern us at present. In social work such codes generally include a statement of the fundamental values of the profession – usually recognisable variations on the themes of respect for persons and user self-determination and frequently some statement of commitment to the promotion of social justice and to professional integrity. This is usually followed by short statements of ethical principles, often with a brief commentary attached. Some are quite detailed, and offer more guidance about how to act in certain types of situation. Others offer general statements of principle with little commentary or specific guidance. They range in size from about two to five pages. Whatever the level of detail, however, probably none would claim that they aim to provide detailed guidance to social workers about how to act in particular situations. The United States code states quite clearly in its preamble:

> In itself, this code does not represent a set of rules that will prescribe all the behaviours of social workers in all the complexities of professional life. Rather, it offers general principles to guide conduct, and the judicious appraisal of conduct, in situations that have ethical implications (NASW 1990).

In attempting to counter criticisms of the code of ethics proposed for BASW, Rice argues that a code of ethics should not attempt detailed guidance, and those who expect this misunderstand the nature of such a code. Those critics who say that the code of ethics will be of no use to a social worker 'confronted by conflicts about Mrs X, with agency Y' are, he claims, seeking a particularity of rules and of guidance 'that would become a substitute for ethical reflection, not a stimulation and illumination of it' (Rice 1975, p. 381). He continues:

> A code of ethics creates the spirit and standard of ethical reflection in that community [of social workers] of ideals, skills and practical concern. A code, over-precise and detailed, would undervalue the professional community ... (ibid).

This point is also echoed by Watson in his reflection on the purpose of the BASW code of ethics 10 years after its introduction (Watson 1985).

Why have a code of ethics?

Although it is often assumed that a code of ethics is a key hallmark of a profession (if one follows the 'trait theory'), Millerson argues that the presence or absence of a code of conduct does not signify professional or non-professional status:

> Some occupations require greater control than others, due to the nature of the work involved. Some need a severe, comprehensive code, others do not. Need for a code depends upon the professional situation (Millerson 1964, p. 9).

Millerson (pp. 151–3) identifies the factors determining the need for introducing a code of ethics as follows:

1. *Type of practice* – a professional working alone in a non-institutional practice would need the guidance of an ethical code much more than an individual in an institutional setting.
2. *Nature of the practice* – if it is based on a so-called 'fiduciary' relationship between the professional and the user, especially trust involving life and property, there is more need for a code.
3. *Technique involved* – if the technique is complex, a code may be necessary to remind the professional to provide the best possible service.

4. *Technical comprehension by users* – where the user cannot be expected to understand the professional's work, a code is required for the protection of the user.
5. *Contact with the user* – if contact is distinct, direct and personal, then it is open to possible abuse, owing to its intimacy. A code therefore protects both professionals and users.
6. *Duty towards the user* – when there is a single user, the duty needs to be clearly defined by a code. With multiple users there is less chance of hiding responsibility (e.g. as with the teacher's responsibility to the child, parents, school authorities, the community, in different ways and for different reasons all at once).

Factors which particularly apply in the case of social work relate to its fiduciary nature (2); the level of comprehension of the user (4) – although this may be less to do with the complexities of the techniques than users' lack of knowledge of social workers' powers and legal duties; and the fact that it involves direct, personal contact with the user, often involving the user giving confidential information (5). The other factors – a non-institutional setting, working with single users and using complex techniques – *may* apply in social work practice, particularly in non-statutory work in private practice, or in specialisms such as family therapy. However, in public sector, generic social work they tend not to apply.

Millerson then goes on to look at the elements that determine the possibility of actually introducing an ethical code. He concludes that it is easier to introduce a code where there is a single form of training leading to qualification, where the professionals concerned are mainly involved in one type of work, and where they work for many employers in a strongly organised and registered profession. Given these factors, it may seem surprising that social work, particularly in Britain where it is not a registered profession and social workers are involved in many different types of activity, actually has a code of ethics. Apart from the factors mentioned above in connection with determining the need for a code of ethics, there are perhaps several other reasons why social work has developed a code of ethics:

1. It is aspiring to be a 'full profession' with comparable status to, say, medicine and the law. Therefore it is felt to be important to have this feature of professionalism to demonstrate professional status and integrity to the public. It can be seen as part of a move towards becoming recognised as a profession. As Wilding (1982, p. 77) suggests:

> codes of ethics are political counters constructed as much to serve as public evidence of professional intentions and ideals as to provide actual behavioural guidelines for practitioners.

2. Equally important, a code of ethics may help to generate a sense of common identity and shared values amongst the occupational group. It may be as much about internal recognition as external. Given that social workers are quite fragmented in terms of the variety of types of work they do and the settings in which they operate, the code of ethics and the values upon which it is based may be the one feature that is held in common.

Comparison of codes of ethics for social work from different countries

In order to study in more depth the nature of codes of ethics in social work, all the professional associations in the 54 countries in membership of the International Federation of Social Workers were written to, requesting a copy of their codes of ethics. Of these, 22 associations replied, eight of which said they did not have a code of their own. Of these eight, three said they were currently using the code of the International Federation of Social Workers (these were Luxembourg, Portugal and Zimbabwe); Iceland reported that a committee was currently working on preparing a code; Spain said it did not have a national code, but sent the code of the Catalonian Association of Social Workers; Hungary said there was not a single professional code for all social workers although many specialist occupational organisations had their own; and Kuwait responded that it had no code as such. Japan sent a statement about the role of social workers, but gave no indication about whether or not there was a code of ethics. Copies of actual codes of ethics were received from 15 associations (including Catalonia), listed in Table 4.1. The Belgian code is that of the French-speaking Association. It is possible that a significant proportion of those countries not responding did not reply because they did not possess a code of ethics. However, the letter requesting information was written in English, and a much higher proportion of English speaking countries and those where English is a common second language replied. So the information from the codes that were obtained cannot be said to be representative of social work worldwide. It simply serves to illustrate our discussion of the nature and purpose of codes of ethics.

Of the 15 professional associations included in Table 4.1, two (Norway and Denmark) sent codes of ethics which were versions of the latest International Federation of Social Workers' code modified slightly to refer to their own countries. The codes of the other associations were all different, though some were obviously derivative of others – for example the Hong Kong code has many similiarities of wording to the United States code, but is not totally the same. Many have been recently revised or created in the 1990s, although Israel's is apparently unchanged since the 1970s. These two factors – that some countries have used codes developed elsewhere and slightly modified or adapted them, and that some versions of codes are much more recent than others – means that differences in the form and content of the codes do not necessarily reflect current differences in social work practice, its legal basis or cultural norms in the various countries. However, there are some interesting similarities and differences between codes, regardless of the reasons for this. The majority of codes start with an initial 'statement of principles' (Britain), 'general principles' (Belgium), 'basic values and beliefs' (Hong Kong), 'philosophy' (Canada) or a 'Foreword' (Sweden) which tends to include statements about respecting the unique value and dignity of every human being, promoting user self-determination, working for social justice and maintaining professional integrity.

Respect for persons and user self-determination

There is a remarkable consistency in the wording of the principle relating to respecting human value and dignity, which usually comes first. For example:

> The social worker holds that: Every human being has a unique dignity irrespective of nationality, ethnicity, social and economic status, gender, sexual preference, age, beliefs, or contribution to society (Australian Association of Social Workers 1989, p. 1).

> Basic to the profession of social work is the recognition of the unique value and dignity of every human being (Irish Association of Social Workers 1986, p. 1).

> All social work assistants and social workers have a duty to respect each individual for his/her inherent dignity and provide his/her professional services without distinction or discrimination in an appropriate way, honouring timetables, appointments and undertakings (Colegio de Asistentes Sociales del Peru 1990, p. 3).

> The social worker respects the individuality of each human being and avoids all forms of discrimination relating, for example, to nationality, sex, age, religion, civil status, political opinions, skin colour, sexual orientation, infirmity or sickness (Association suisse des assistants sociaux diplômés et des éducateurs spécialisés 1990, p. 3).

As can be seen from Table 4.1 all codes contain some variation of this basic principle of respect for persons. Most also make reference to the promotion of user self-determination in their statements of general principles (although the term 'client' rather than 'user' tends to be used in most codes). The codes vary,

Table 4.1   *Comparison of codes of ethics from different countries*

Country	Date	General principles				Range of duties	Professional practice issues
		(1)	(2)	(3)	(4)		
Australia	1989	yes	yes	yes	yes	no	yes
Belgium (F)	1985	yes	yes	yes	pt	no	no
Britain	1986	yes	yes	yes	yes	no	no
Canada	1983	yes	yes	yes	yes	yes	yes
Denmark	1993	yes	yes	yes	yes	no	no
France	1981	yes	yes	no	yes	yes	pt
Hong Kong	1993	yes	yes	yes	yes	yes	yes
Ireland	1986	yes	yes	yes	yes	no	no
Israel	1978	yes	pt	no	yes	yes	no
Norway	1993	yes	yes	yes	yes	no	no
Peru	1990	yes	yes	pt	yes	yes	pt
Spain (Cat.)	1988	yes	yes	yes	yes	yes	no
Sweden	1991	yes	yes	yes	yes	yes	no
Switzerland	1990	yes	yes	yes	yes	yes	yes
USA	1990	yes	yes	yes	yes	yes	yes

Notes

General principles: does the code include the following principles – yes, no or partly (pt)?

(1) Respect for the unique value of the individual person
(2) User self-determination
(3) Social justice
(4) Professional integrity

Range of duties: does the code divide the responsibilities of the social worker into at least three of the following – those to users, agency, colleagues, society, profession?

Professional practice issues: does the code cover some professional practice issues such as guidance or rules on advertising, charging fees, user access to records, using clients in research, etc.?

however, in the extent to which this principle is developed in the further guidance or principles of practice through, for example, advocating shared control between user and worker (Canadian Association of Social Workers 1983, p. 4), participation of users in ensuring and defining appropriate services (BASW 1986, p. 2), or giving precedence to the users' own definitions of their situations (Swedish Union of Social Workers (SSR) 1991, p. iv). In some codes, such as those of Hong Kong and the United States, such explicit statements about user participation and control do not seem to be included over and above the general statement about social workers fostering maximum self-determination on the part of users. Indeed, the US code focusses under this heading mainly on cases where the social worker is acting on behalf of a user and also stresses that the civil and legal rights of the user should not be violated. There is little evidence of positive commitment to empower users, more a concern that their rights should be protected (negative freedom). However, at the end of the code, under the heading of promotion of the general welfare, some statements are made about the social worker acting to expand choice and opportunity for all persons.

Social justice and professional integrity

Another feature of most codes is a statement that the social worker should have a commitment to social justice, although these exact words may not be used. For example, the British code states:

> The worker has the right and duty to bring to the attention of those in power, and of the general public, ways in which the activities of government, society or agencies create or contribute to hardship and suffering or militate against their relief (BASW 1986, p. 2).

The Catalonian code states that it is an ethical duty of social workers to

> support the development of laws and policy changes which will improve social conditions and help preserve social justice, and secure the participation of the people concerned (Collegi Oficial de Diplomats en Treball Social i Assistents Socials de Catalunya 1988, p. 16).

The Australian code stands out in that it stresses the social worker's commitment to social justice, stating that the social worker should:

> advocate changes in policy, service delivery and social conditions which enhance the opportunities for those most vulnerable in the community (AASW 1989, p. 2).

The achievement of social justice is said to be 'co-equal with the attainment of fulfilment for the individual' (ibid., p. 1). This may well be the intention in some of the other codes, but it is certainly not stated so clearly in any of the others, where statements such as 'the social worker has a primary responsibility to users' (Hong Kong Social Welfare Personnel Registration Council 1993, p. 1) or 'I will regard the well-being of the persons I serve as my primary professional obligation' (Canadian Association of Social Workers 1983, p. 3) imply that the social worker's first responsibility is to the welfare of the individual users.

The Swedish code is interesting in the way in which it advocates the pursuit of social justice when it states that the social worker shall, 'with her knowledge and experience, contribute to a development in society that promotes peace, freedom, equality and social justice' (SSR 1991, p. viii). The Swedish code continues:

> The professional responsibilities of the social worker are not limited to her own work and her own place of work. The social worker shares the resonsibility with other social workers to strive for the fulfilment of the values laid down in these ethical guidelines for professional social work. This responsibility is neither limited to their own national society, the country. Wheresoever social and other injustice occurs, the social worker has a responsibility to fight them (ibid).

This statement goes beyond merely a concern with the social worker in the role of a responsible professional, to the social worker as a *person*. It is almost suggesting that the person who chooses to become a social worker is (or should be) a special kind of person, one who has a vocation or calling to work for a better society. The fundamental values of the social work profession – the promotion of individual freedom and social justice – do not just apply to the person when in the role of social worker, when at work; they must be a part of the whole person. In effect, the Swedish code seems to be suggesting that to distinguish between personal and professional values, between the person in the role of social worker and the person in everyday life, is not possible (or should not be possible). Indeed, the second basic principle of the Swedish code is: 'The social worker shall in her professional practice and in her life at large respect the equal value of each human being' (op. cit., p. iii). The commentary on this statement says 'The ethics of professional life should be in accordance with the ethics of her [the social worker's] life as a whole' (ibid). This contrasts markedly with some of the other codes which acknowledge, or even advocate, a ' clear separation between personal and professional life: 'The private conduct of the social worker is a personal matter to the same degree as is any other person's, except when such conduct compromises the fulfillment of professional responsibilities' (NASW 1990, p. 3).

Indeed, the majority of the codes (including the Swedish) contain statements to the effect that social workers should always make it clear when making public statements or undertaking public activities whether they are acting in a personal or professional capacity. Some of the complex issues relating to the separation and interrelationship of the personal and professional will be returned to later. This is just one of the differences in emphasis between the various codes, which may reflect differences in national culture and perceptions of the role of social workers, or simply the idealism of the members of the professional association drawing up the code. It is perhaps pertinent that in Sweden the profession of social work is not legally protected (therefore presumably the professional association is not having to put this code into practice when disciplining its members) and the incidence of private practice (where fees as opposed to a salary from the state are the basis of the worker's job) is low. A commitment to a strong, caring welfare state as an expression of collective altruism, of which the social worker is a part, may be a more dominant ideal in Swedish society than in many others where the role of the welfare state is less all-embracing and hence more obviously focussed on the control functions. The greater interpenetration of the welfare state into personal life in Sweden – with its highly developed child care and benefit systems (Gould 1988) – may discourage the separation of the personal and professional that seems so obvious and necessary in other countries.

All codes also lay great stress on what is often termed 'professional integrity'. Indeed, this could be said to be the whole purpose of a code of ethics – to affirm publicly the commitment of members of the profession to act in a manner befitting their knowledge and status in society. This includes taking responsibility for their actions and ensuring they are in line with the code, a commitment to the continuing development of their knowledge and skills, not using their special knowledge and skills for inhuman purposes, not abusing the relative power-lessness of the user through having sexual relationships, not bringing into disrepute the good name of the profession through malpractice, and monitoring and challenging agency policies and practices which may be contrary to the ethical code. However, the codes vary in the extent to which they clearly and unequivocally state that the professional code must take priority over agency rules and procedures. For example, the Canadian code states: 'if a conflict arises in professional practice, the standards declared in this code take precedence' (CASW 1983, p. 3). Whereas the British code simply calls upon social workers to work for 'the creation and maintenance in employing agencies of conditions which enable social workers to accept the obligations of this code' (BASW 1986, p. 3).

Range of duties

Some codes are also much clearer than others about the potential for conflict between different principles and duties (for example, duties to the agency or to society as opposed to the promotion of the user's interests). The International Federation of Social Workers' 1993 code (which is used by Norway and Denmark) includes a separate section entitled 'problem areas' which itemises areas of potential conflicting interests, and also mentions the problems of the dual function of social worker as carer and controller. This is perhaps the clearest statement about the potential for conflict of all the codes. However, the IFSW code, partly no doubt because it is intended to apply universally, does not give any guidance regarding how to solve such conflicts. Some codes, although not the IFSW one, probably for the reasons just mentioned, are actually laid out in a format which itemises in turn the social worker's responsibility to users, colleagues, employers and employing organisations, the profession and to society. The US code is a good example of this, and many others are also laid out in this way, although some do not separately itemise responsibility to society. This does seem a very helpful format, because it acknowledges that the social worker has a range of duties to a variety of interest groups. The British code, for example, while acknowledging in one sentence in its foreword that members of a profession have 'obligations to their clients, to their employers, to each other, to colleagues in other disciplines and to society' (BASW 1986, p. 1) does not go on to specify clearly what these different obligations are and what to do when they conflict.

Professional practice issues

This links with the different levels of detail and guidance offered by the codes. The Canadian code is probably the most detailed, giving some very specific guidance including, for example, a detailed specification of the knowledge and skills it is the social worker's duty to possess, when educational degrees can be cited, how the self-employed social worker should disclose charges at the beginning of a relationship or what to do when disclosure of confidential information is required by order of a court. It is at this point that the code of ethics, or statement of general principles and general guidance, begins to merge into what we earlier called a 'code of practice'. Some codes state nothing about matters such as advertising of qualifications or setting reasonable levels of fees (see Table 4.1 under the heading of 'professional practice issues'); others make some general statements, but not at the level of detail of the Canadian code. For example, the US code makes a statement about fees as follows:

> When setting fees, the social worker should ensure that they are fair, reasonable, considerate, and commensurate with the service performed and with due regard for the clients' ability to pay (NASW 1990, p. 6).

Whereas the Canadian code gives much more detailed guidance, for example:

> The self-employed social worker's bill will reflect only services actually rendered and reasonable penalties for appointments missed or cancelled without adequate notice from the client (CAWS 1983, p. 8).

Obviously issues about fees and advertising are pertinant in countries where private practice is commonplace. Elsewhere, as in Britain, it may not be thought necessary to include these matters in a code of ethics. The extent to which such detailed codes of practice are appropriate and enforceable will also depend upon whether the profession of social work is legally recognised in a country and whether the professional association (or some other regulatory body) has established committees and procedures for hearing complaints, making investigations into breaches of the code, and disciplining members through fines, suspension or termination of membership. The Australian code of ethics, for example, is published in a booklet which also includes the association's 'by-laws on ethics' detailing the mechanisms for appointing national and local committees on ethical and professional standards, how complaints and appeals should be made and dealt with, and what sanctions can be applied. The Swiss code includes a page outlining procedures in cases of infringements of the code and the measures and sanctions that can be taken by the Commission on professional ethics. In Britain, however, there is no known case of a member of the British Association of Social Workers having been disciplined by the association for breach of the ethical code. Not all social workers belong to BASW anyway. The situation in Britain is further complicated by the fact that the title of 'social worker' is not legally protected – that is, there is no register of qualified social workers and therefore no nationally recognised system of stiking off the register those practitioners deemed to have acted incompetently or unethically. Further, unqualified people can be described as 'social workers'.

Recently there have been proposals to establish a General Council for Social Work and a register, along the lines of the

British Medical Council (Rickford 1992; Ivory 1993). These proposals seem particularly necessary to many in the profession in the light of recent public outcrys relating to malpractices by residential child care workers, and several cases of social workers either over-reacting or under-reacting to risks of child abuse. It has been argued that the establishment of a General Council for Social Work would serve to protect the public as well as enhancing the reputation of social work. Although the role of keeping the register of qualified practitioners and striking off practitioners would not be that of the professional association, there is no doubt that the role of the professional association would be enhanced (rather similar to the role of the British Medical Association) in that it would also take independent ethical sanctions against its members, as well as offering them protection when unjustly accused of malpractice. This appears to be the role of the professional associations in those countries where the title of qualified social worker is legally protected. In fact, in all European Community countries except Ireland, Italy and Britain, the title of social worker is protected by law (IFSW 1989). It is only in these three countries and the Netherlands that it is possible for an unqualified person to be described in the same way as a qualified person. Having a legally protected title and a register of qualified practitioners is obviously another important move in social work towards the status of a more exclusive professionalism. It is partly for this reason that some of the trade unions representing people who work in the field of social work (both qualified and unqualified) have argued against the proposals, suggesting that it is a further move towards elitism and protectionism and will divide the occupation into qualified and unqualified (see the discussion in Cohen 1990).

The function of a professional code of ethics in bureaucracies

Having examined the content of the various codes of ethics, we will now explore the extent to which such codes can actually be used by social workers in their daily practice. It has sometimes been argued that social workers, and other welfare professionals, are not 'autonomous' in the same way as members of the established professions are. The example often given is that of medicine, where doctors are 'free' to make their own professional judgements about the needs and requirements of their patients without reference to outside hierarchies or bureaucrats. However, social work is frequently practised in bureaucratic organisations, and there is a tension between the ideal of professional autonomy, and the reality of a rule-governed, hierarchical structure. As Toren states:

> One of the main features of a bureaucratic organisation is that the work of its members is directed by a set of universalistic rules and procedures. These can be maintained only if the work done is specific and routine; the helping professions, and in particular social work, are neither (Toren 1972, p. 57).

She argues that the approach of social workers to users (which would be in accordance with the codes of ethics as well as their education and training) is to treat them as whole people, taking account of all of their needs; and also to see them as unique – in which case there will always be special circumstances, or exceptions to the rule. So the primacy of the ethical code, which professionals are supposed to apply according to their own judgements, is challenged by the clearly defined organisational rules and supervision or line management of a bureaucracy.

While there is obviously some truth in this, it can be questioned whether the distinction is as clear and straightforward as has been made out. We might question whether doctors working in a state-funded hospital, or a lawyer employed by a large law firm, are really completely autonomous or free from control from their superiors (Toren 1972, p. 53). Talcott Parsons (1959) outlined a system of dual authority which could be applied to a hospital: the administrative system which is concerned with the organisation as a whole – patient numbers, financial matters, recruitment of staff; and the operative system, which is concerned with implementing the organisation's goals, that is, treating patients. A hospital could be characterised as what Mintzberg calls a 'professional bureaucracy'. Mintzberg makes quite a useful distinction between what he calls 'machine bureaucracies' which rely on authority of a hierarchical nature, and 'professional bureaucracies' which allow for participative decision-making by the 'frontline' staff with less hierarchy imposed over them (Mintzberg 1979). In professional bureaucracies standardisation or quality of output is not controlled by direct supervision, but by 'professional' standards, learnt through training and experience, and regulated by professional bodies and peer pressure from outside any one organisation. Individual staff work largely autonomously with little need for direct supervision. Examples might be universities, hospitals, social work and other human service agencies (Bloxham 1993).

However, while it may be appropriate to describe many of the organisational settings in which social work is practised as professional bureaucracies, arguably social workers do not have as much control over their own work or as much professional respect and status as doctors or university lecturers; also the local authority structures in which many social workers still work in Britain are traditionally quite hierarchical and rule-bound. While it may be argued that the concept and practice of 'supervision' in social work is as much about personal development and support in an emotionally demanding job as it is about management, close supervision is nevertheless enshrined in social work and it is largely carried out by people in a managerial role (although usually qualified social workers). Traditional local authority procedures often demand, for example, that individual social workers cannot even sign their own letters, which must all go out under the signature of the area manager or divisional director. It could still be argued that there is less scope for social workers employed in bureaucratic organisations to retain as large a degree of professional autonomy as other professionals such as doctors who also work in bureaucracies, or as social workers working in less bureaucratic structures in small independent or private agencies. This would seem to imply there might be less scope for retaining professional identity and upholding the code of ethics as a primary obligation to the profession. There are currently changes taking place in the management and structure of social work in Britain and in other countries which are resulting in both more responsibility being devolved to social workers (for example, by managing budgets) yet also in the centralising and proceduralising of more of the tasks undertaken by social workers. The implications of this will be discussed later.

It may be more useful to explore which aspects of a professional's practice are controlled, by whom and how, than it is to try to categorise professions in terms of which are autonomous and which are not. Toren argues that the encounter between the social worker and user is usually not observable and is therefore not directly controllable, which allows the social worker a great degree of autonomy in relation to contacts with users. Yet many other aspects of the job are much more controlled, such as the distribution of resources and services to users. It is these aspects of the job that are subject to bureaucratic procedures as opposed to professional standards. This is reflected in the fact that most codes of ethics are more concerned with how the social worker should treat the individual user than they are with prescribing how resources should be allocated between users, which might seem to be an agency or governmental matter.

Yet while in theory it may be possible to separate out the pure encounter with the user from the bureaucratic controls and procedures of the agency, in practice it is the rules of the agency which define who is to be regarded as a user and provide the context in which the social worker operates. They already define the *person* who approaches the social work agency for help, or who is approached by the agency offering help, surveillance or control, as a *service user* and the kind of help that can be given or control required. Within this context the social worker has some freedom to treat the user in the way she or he thinks fit. Yet this is limited, and is currently being even further limited in Britain as the government and social work agencies develop many more sets of procedures and rules regarding how to carry out the work. This trend is happening not only in social work, but also in the older established professions of medicine and the law, as part of a challenge to the autonomy and power of professionals. There is also a trend towards the fragmentation of social work into specialisms and multi-disciplinary work, which again tends to result in a loss of professional identity. This appears to be happening across Europe and was noted by Thérèse Rossel at a seminar in 1990 when she noted:

> ... the movement towards the administrative decentralisation of social services on the one hand; and the introduction into work and to projects or programmes of notions such as multi-disciplinary and community development (IFSW 1990, p. 27).

She suggested that these changes were responsible for 'the fragmentation of the profession, and the dangers of a loss of identity'. The International Federation of Social Workers recommended therefore:

> that to develop, at an European level, the values on which social work depends in our respective countries constitutes a professional obligation, articulated in the International Code of Ethics. This code is the proper expression of values which must, here and now, guide social work and social action (ibid., p. 29).

The code of ethics is seen to be a unifying factor which may help to hold together the profession at a time of fragmentation. Yet, equally, it could be argued that professional codes of ethics may become increasingly irrelevant if this trend continues and the occupational identity of 'social worker' begins to crumble. We noted earlier Millerson's view that it is difficult to introduce a code of ethics if there is not one main dominating kind of work. If there are lots of different specialisms (child protection, community care, mental health, family therapy, welfare rights, case management) in different agency settings (public, private, independent, voluntary) this may mean there is an even greater need for a code of ethics to hold the profession together, while at the same time it becomes more difficult to maintain the code as important, relevant and a primary source of moral guidance. Certainly there will be very different codes of practice, and arguably the agency rules and procedures will be more influential than a set of general moral principles published by the professional association.

How useful are codes of ethics?

Some commentators are sceptical about the value of codes of ethics. This is not just because of their link with the evolution of an occupation towards professional exclusivity and elitism (Wilding 1982). Downie and Calman (1987) when examining codes of ethics in health care identify a number of limitations:

1. The codes tend to imply that professionals are given their ethics, whereas it is at least as true that professionals bring with them their own individual values.
2. Many aspects of welfare and caring work are not expressible in terms of rules or duties – for example the cultivation of certain attitudes such as compassion.
3. Codes tend to be exclusive to one profession, whereas welfare and caring work is now increasingly provided by multi-disciplinary teams.
4. Codes assume an exclusive professional–user relationship, with the professionals doing the best they can for the individual users; this ignores the pressing economic considerations in welfare and caring work.
5. Codes assume a consensus on values both within the professions and their public. But it is doubtful whether this still exists, as professions are fragmented and users are increasingly demanding that services are delivered in terms of their own values rather than those of the professions. As Downie and Calman comment:

> To the extent that the professions are now expected to work *through* the community rather than *on* it, the position of codes of

ethics has shifted from the centre of professional life to the margins (Downie and Calman 1987, p. 244).

Indeed, many social workers are also rather sceptical about the value of a code of ethics. How useful a code of ethics is, depends upon what one wants to use it for. While many of Downie and Calman's criticisms are very valid, we need to recognise that a professional code performs a number of different functions, one of which may be an attempt to maintain professional power and identity at a time when these are threatened. We have already noted that there are a number of reasons why a profession may have a code of ethics, including:

1. to contribute to the 'professional status' of an occupation
2. to establish and maintain professional identity
3. to guide practitioners about how to act
4. to protect users from malpractice or abuse.

The first two reasons relate to the occupation of social work as a whole, and are about perceptions and identity rather than directly about practice. They are about how the outside world sees social work, and how social workers view themselves. Of course, if it is effectively to fulfil the first two aims, the code must relate to social work practice and be known about by members of the profession. But such a code can be quite general in nature; indeed, it is probably helpful if it is general – consisting of statements of values or general moral principles that can be accepted by all members of the occupation. It is this kind of function that the International Federation of Social Workers sees for its code at a time of change and fragmentation within the occupation. Arguably this is also the main role played by many of the more general codes, such as the British, Irish, or Swedish.

However, most of the codes include other aims or purposes, particularly (3) guiding social workers and (4) protecting users. How effectively can they do this? Regarding guidance to social workers, the effectiveness of this will depend upon what social workers expect. If they are looking for detailed guidance on how to act in particular situations, then they will usually be disappointed. As was stated earlier, this would both be impossible, given the complexity of social work practice, and would also contradict a key feature of what it means to be a professional – namely that education and a commitment to a set of values enable professionals to make their own (autonomous) informed and considered judgements on professional matters. If the code of ethics was to be turned into a detailed rulebook, then the social worker would merely have to follow it unthinkingly, and there would be no room for discretion and judgement.

On the other hand, while recognising that ethical codes cannot and should not be detailed rulebooks, it could be argued that they frequently consist of a set of principles of such a general nature as to be open to wide interpretation and are therefore useless in guiding practice. We suggested in chapter 2 how user self-determination, for example, could be interpreted as meaning anything from leaving the user completely alone, to justifying parentalist intervention to increase the user's capacities for self-determined action. The codes, to be successful in their aims of guiding practitioners even in a general way, probably need to be related more clearly to practice than many in fact are. One way of doing this is to ensure that the general value statements are discussed and analysed during the course of social work training and related to the daily practice of social work. Otherwise the codes of ethics are left hanging in a vacuum, or sitting in a drawer, unused and unusable. Another way in which they can be related to practice is by including codes of practice alongside the codes of ethics (as is the case in the Canadian code). The problem with the development of more detailed codes of practice at a national level by the professional association alongside the codes of ethics is that they can be over-prescriptive and do not allow for variations in work contexts and user groups in which some of the 'rules' or guidance may not apply. While it may be appropriate for the Law Society in Britain to devise detailed codes of conduct relating to the minutiae of fees or advertising, in social work such a project seems much more problematic.

What is happening, however, is that most agencies are developing their own codes of practice for dealing with specific issues, especially relating to the user's rights – such as confidentiality, access to records, or making complaints. Obviously these will vary from agency to agency, but such codes of practice seem much more clearly designed to protect and clarify users' rights and to clarify the roles of the social worker and the agency. What is important is that these codes of practice are related clearly to the more general value statements in the codes of ethics and can be seen to be a development from them. The most appropriate statement that might be made about confidentiality, for example, in a national code of ethics might be that social workers should ensure that their agencies have policies and codes of practice clearly stating the extent to which information given by the user to a social worker will and will not be kept confidential. Obviously the extent to which information can be kept confidential may be very different in an independent counselling agency, compared with a statutory child protection agency. Therefore the role of the code of ethics in guiding practice seems to be to outline the broad principles of the profession and the potential areas where ethical issues will arise.

Regarding the role of a code of ethics in protecting the user, this can only be fulfilled in a very general way in laying down broad principles relating to respect, non-exploitation or abuse. Yet these should be obvious anyway, and it is the more subtle and detailed use of power and knowledge from which the user may need some protection. Perhaps this can also be better served (though still very imperfectly) through well-publicised and clear agency codes of practice regarding such issues as making contracts with users, procedures for access to records, or rights to complaint. The next chapter will explore further the concept of codes of practice and their relationship to codes of ethics.

Conclusions

In this chapter we have examined the nature and function of codes of ethics in social work. We noted that the existence of codes of ethics for social work is intimately related to the notion of professionalism, and one of their main functions is to maintain professional status and identity. In looking at codes of ethics developed by professional associations in different countries, many common features were noted, particularly a congruence around the stated values or principles underpinning social work including: respect for the individual person, promotion of user self-determination, promotion of social justice and working for the interests of users. The extent to which the codes acknowledge that the societal and agency contexts in which social work is practised may also place demands on social workers varies, as does the level of detail regarding practical guidance on matters such as charging fees, advertising qualifications or user access to records.

The extent to which social workers regard such codes as useful will depend upon what they want to use them for. For practical guidance on how to act in certain types of situations and as a means of safeguarding users' rights, agency codes of practice may be more useful. However, as a means of defending the profession from outside attack, of maintaining professional identity and of setting some general benchmarks against which to judge agency policies and practice they do have a role to play. The codes emphasise that social workers have a responsibility over and above just doing the job and following the agency's rules. This may be useful at a time when resources for social work are being reduced and standards of work and the quality of service may be threatened. The codes of ethics remind social workers that because they possess particular knowledge and skills, and work on a daily basis with people living in poverty and suffering crises and problems, they have a duty to inform governments and agencies of inequities, lack of resources or the need for policy changes. Yet, because of the changes in the management and delivery of social services, codes of ethics are also becoming increasingly irrelevant, with their emphasis on professionally defined values (as opposed to those defined by the users), their assumption of a professional consensus (when much work is specialised and multi-disciplinary) and their focus on service to users (in a climate where economy and efficiency are also of prime importance). In such a climate, codes of practice developed by social work agencies are more important ways of safeguarding user rights. Social workers still need to be prepared to challenge agency policies and practices and to view themselves as more than just employees doing a job. The code of ethics, along with education and training, obviously has a role to play in this.

5

Users' Rights: Codes of Practice and the New Consumerism

In the last chapter we argued that the main role of codes of ethics is to establish and maintain professional identity. Although they claim to play a role in protecting the interests and rights of users and in guiding social workers, this is an indirect role. The general principles in the codes of ethics cannot immediately and obviously be put into practice. They must be interpreted and translated into some more specific principles or guidance. In this chapter we will look at what is meant by 'rights', the difference between regarding the user as a person, a citizen or a consumer, the growing trend towards developing procedures and codes of practice which state and protect users' rights, and the approaches that need to be adopted by social workers to enable users to exercise these rights.

Rights

There are many different political and philosophical theories regarding what is a right, where rights come from and whether they are regarded as the basic category of morality. I will suggest a view which I think makes sense in the context of this book and which probably reflects how rights tend to be regarded in western society in general and social work in particular. Rights are generally regarded as belonging to individuals, although this view does not necessarily make sense in societies where the individual person is not the prime focus of cultural norms and ways of life. Rights are an important part of the western liberal tradition in politics and moral philosophy, which we have already linked to the Kantian notion of respect for persons. If respect for persons is regarded as the ultimate principle of morality, or indeed a precondition for any morality whatsoever, then it follows that persons have certain rights which should be respected.

According to Feinberg (1973, p. 64) a right is a valid claim. By 'valid' he means justified according to a system of rules. If someone has a right, then at least one other person must have duties towards that person. He elucidates the concept of a right with reference to a claim, arguing that a right is more than just a claim. Whereas claims may differ in degree (some may be stronger than others), rights do not. Whereas claims may be invalid, rights cannot be. He gives the example of young orphans throughout the world needing a good upbringing, including a balanced diet. He argues that this is a claim, not a right, because in many places resources are not available and therefore no particular person has a duty to provide goods. This definition of rights obviously has implications for how we regard some of the 'rights' included in the United Nations Universal Declaration of the Rights of the Child: for example, the right of all children to 'adequate nutrition, housing, recreation and medical services' (1959, principle 4). Feinberg regards the use of the term 'human rights' in the UN and other similar declarations as a 'special manifesto sense of right' which identifies basic needs with rights. He argues that such statements should more properly be described as urging on the world community the moral principle that all basic human needs ought to be recognised as 'claims worthy of sympathy and serious consideration now, even though they cannot yet plausibly be treated as valid claims' (Feinberg 1973, p. 67).

Having defined rights as valid claims, we should now explore different types of rights. The distinction is often made between negative and positive rights as follows:

- **Negative rights** (or liberties) relate to the freedom to do something without interference (for example, free speech);

- **Positive rights** (claim rights) claim against someone else to do something (for example, medical treatment).

Another distinction is that between legal rights and moral rights, and both of these can be either positive or negative:

- **A legal right** is a valid claim by virtue of the legal code or customary practice (for example, the right to vote);
- **A moral right** is a valid claim bestowed by a moral code (for example, the right to be treated with honesty).

These two categories are not mutually exclusive, as many moral rights are also legal rights (for example the right to free speech).

There are two further important distinctions between types of rights: absolute (or unqualifed) rights and conditional (or qualified) rights; and universal rights (applying to everybody without exception) and particular rights (applying to a limited class of people). Clark with Asquith (1985, p. 24) draw up a useful table relating to the four possible combinations of rights in these categories, from which the following list is derived:

1. **Absolute universal rights** – apply unconditionally to everybody. Clark with Asquith argue that there is probably only one right in this category, and that would be the right to be treated as an end and not simply as a means (which logically follows from the concept of respect for persons).
2. **Qualified universal rights** – apply to everybody, except they may be withdrawn from anybody on the basis of the application of criteria which apply to all. This category would include those rights that have often been put forward as 'natural rights' (that is, rights simply deducible from the nature of humankind) and some of what are included as 'human rights', such as the right to liberty, which can be withheld on certain grounds. For example, the right to liberty is suspended for the imprisoned criminal.
3. **Absolute particular rights** – apply without qualification to everybody in a certain category. For example, all parents who are British citizens have an absolute right to claim child benefit.

4. **Qualified particular rights** – apply to certain persons under certain conditions. For example, a British citizen has a right to a state pension if over the prescribed retirement age and having satisfied the necessary contribution conditions.

The question as to whether there are any basic universal human needs and any universal moral rights links to questions of cultural imperialism and moral relativism and is much debated (see Outka and Reeder 1993, and the discussion in chapter 2 about the dominance of an ethic of justice). In relation to social work it is important to note that the International Federation of Social Workers certainly believes in the existence of universal moral rights and endorses as part of its code of ethics the UN Declarations of Human Rights and the Rights of the Child.

Clark with Asquith (1975, p. 27) argue that social workers mainly deal with qualified particular rights on a day-to-day basis and the 'application of universal rights cannot, without absurdity, be essentially different in social work from any other context'. However, the statements of values and ethics made by the social work profession invariably focus on what appear to be regarded as either absolute or qualified *universal rights*.

Clark with Asquith produce a typical list of users' rights drawn from the social work literature as follows:

1. to be treated as an end
2. to self-determination
3. to be accepted for what one is
4. to be treated as a unique individual
5. to non-discrimination on irrelevant grounds
6. to treatment on the principles of honesty, openness and non-deception
7. to have information given to the worker in the course of social work treatment treated as confidential
8. to a professionally competent service
9. to access to resources for which there exists an entitlement ('welfare rights').

The first six rights on the list could be said to be derived from the principle of respect for persons, and are very similar to the list produced by Biestek discussed in chapter 2. The first right is an absolute universal right, and (2) to (5) could be regarded as qualified universal rights. The right to welfare (9) could be said to relate to users as citizens of a specific country; the welfare rights may be universal in that country (the right to health care) or more usually in Britain particular (the right of parents to child benefit). The right to confidentiality (7) and a professionally competent service (8) refer specifically to someone in the role of a social work user and therefore are particular. Confidentiality is qualified, as there are rules regarding when one is allowed to break confidentiality (for example, when someone else's rights or interests are seriously threatened, or if it is in the user's interests). The right to a professionally competent service is, arguably, an unqualified right. It may be the case that a professionally competent service is not delivered due to lack of qualified staff as a result of resource constraints. However, this should not negate the user's right to that standard of service.

The user as a person

Such lists, like those of Biestek and the others highlighted in Table 2.1, focus more on the universal rights which should apply to all people, than on the particular rights applying to the service user *qua* user. The emphasis on the social work user as a **person** with the basic moral rights derived from the principle of respect for persons was the dominant one in the social work literature until perhaps the last 15 years. This meant that the kinds of moral principles stated for social work were no different to the kinds of moral principles that would be stated for morality in general, although the context in which they were applied obviously presented specific issues and difficulties for workers. This type of view based on Kantian philosophy and Biestek's list of casework principles has already been discussed in the section on the principles of the social worker–user relationship in chapter 2.

The user as a citizen

In the late 1970s and early 1980s the notion of 'clients as fellow citizens' began to be stressed (Jordan 1975; BASW 1980) as part of the reaction against the view of the social worker as expert giving psychological explanations of users' problems, and as a move towards regarding social workers as allies of users (Payne 1989, p. 121). Studies had been published (e.g. Mayer and Timms 1970) relating to users' views of social work which contributed to the pressure to alter the power balance between users and social workers. As Phelan commented: 'As social workers we have a responsibility to bear constantly in mind that our clients are equal with us. They have complete citizenship' (BASW 1980).

This kind of view entails that the rights of users should be seen as rights of citizens not to be treated arbitrarily by state officials, and therefore as having rights of access to information about the purpose of social work, to see personal information held by social work agencies on file, and to participate in planning and decision-making, for example. The principle of respecting the user as a fellow citizen could be regarded as a development of the idea of respect for persons. However, the term 'citizen' is narrower than 'person', in that it focusses on the rights of the person in the role of citizen, rather than respect for the person as a person. Citizenship entails more specific rights, including social rights to the benefits and services of the welfare state, as well as political and civil rights. The 'user as fellow citizen' approach therefore increases the accountability of social workers, although it is reductive in its view of the user.

The term 'citizen' is as contested as many of the others we have been using. The notion of the user as a fellow citizen will be interpreted differently depending on how citizenship is construed – whether in terms of the liberal tradition of individual rights, social citizenship with a stress on reciprocity and common interests (Jordan 1989), or citizenship based on meeting people's needs (Taylor 1989). The idea of users as fellow citizens suggests that both social workers and users are members of a common community or society and as such possess certain rights. If we follow T. H. Marshall, these could be described as political (for example, the right to vote), civil (for example, the right to freedom of speech), and social (for example, the right to education). According to Marshall citizenship is: 'a status bestowed on those who are full members of a community. All those who possess the status are equal with respect to the rights and duties with which the status is endowed' (Marshall 1963, p. 87).

This implies that these rights and duties apply equally to everyone. Yet as Taylor has argued, citizenship, with its notions of membership of a community (particularly a nation) is based on a set of practices which excludes certain people from full membership. He gives as an example the Immigration Act 1988 which rules that the wives of British and Commonwealth men settled in Britain can only be brought into the country if they can be supported themselves and will have no recourse to public funds. There are many other ways in which some people are denied full citizenship rights, particularly women, Black people, people with disabilities, lesbians and gays and children (Taylor 1989; Lister 1991). It is likely that a significant number of the people who become users of social work services may not have or may not be able to exercise full citizenship rights. While social workers may believe that everyone in society *ought* to have equal status, and it may be a good principle for the social worker to regard the users as fellow citizens, there is no point in pretending that this is the case in our present society. Users are often people who have been excluded from the political process (for example, with no address they cannot vote), and who do not share in the rights and benefits associated with employment. Social workers do not have the power to make people fellow citizens. However, the services and contact offered by social workers can treat people in a way fellow citizens ought to be treated – that is, users should not be stigmatised, or treated as undeserving. This relates to the discussion at the end of chapter 3 where it was suggested that users could be treated with respect, within a framework of societal and agency constraints.

Social work, as part of social services, is one of the institutions responsible for delivering what Marshall called 'the right to welfare' or social rights. Social rights include the right to education, a state pension, and many other rights, some of which social workers may be regarded as contributing to, ranging from: 'modicum of economic welfare and security to the right to share to the full in the social heritage and to live the life of a civilised being according to the standards prevailing in society' (Marshall 1963, p. 74).

Some of these rights are enshrined in law (such as education), others are what might be described as moral rights (such as the right to live the life of a civilised human being). The fact that these are all described as rights of citizenship means that those who receive benefits or services through the welfare state should regard them as their's of right, that is, they should not be regarded as dependent or stigmatised, and should not be treated arbitrarily by state officials (Campbell 1978). This obviously poses a challenge for social work. Many of the people seeking social work help, or required to have contact with social workers, may have been already denied full citizenship rights, and/or may find it difficult to exercise their rights due to poverty, lack of confidence, or lack of competence, for example. They may feel they do not have a genuine right to services, or they do not have the power or confidence to complain if the services are inadequate. Except in areas of social work which are subject to the law, such as child protection, mental health, or probation work, there have not been clear rules or guidelines about who should be offered social work help and what the nature of the help should be. This has made it doubly difficult for users to complain or appeal about the service received from social workers. Campbell suggests that social workers have exercised considerable discretionary powers over users based on their professional judgement of what is in the user's best interests. He suggests that the user's rights to social work help or consideration are discretionary, which makes it very difficult to appeal against the treatment or service received. One of the ways in which user's rights as citizens can be made more real is if they are given more information about the service offered, the right to appeal, and treated more as equals rather than needy recipients of welfare handouts and social work advice. As Marshall said: 'the right of appeal helps keep alive the idea that the granting of assistance is not a fact of grace, but the satisfaction of a right' (Marshall 1963, p. 89).

The user as consumer

The notion of the service user as a 'consumer' possessing quite specific rights to be treated in a certain kind of way and to receive a certain standard of service is an even further narrowing down, or arguably a move away from, the concept of a person with universal rights. This has developed in the 1980s and 1990s as part of the growth of charterised standards and quality assurance indicators. One of the aims, particularly of the Conservative government in Britain, of adopting the terminology of consumers (or 'customers') is to emphasise the notion of *choice*. Although customers are people who receive services, they are able to choose between the services on offer. If they do not like a particular service, they are free to go elsewhere. They exert some power in exercising this choice and are therefore not merely passive recipients. This model is obviously based on the traditional idea of the market place, with sellers of goods and services competing with each other to find buyers. The buyers will be looking for services that meet their particular needs, offering the level of quality desired, at the right price. Such a notion has not traditionally been applied to the services provided by the welfare state – largely because there has usually been a monopoly supplier, the state, and although it would make sense to say that people's welfare rights entitled them to a certain standard of service, it was usually difficult for them to 'take their custom elsewhere'. With the introduction of 'quasi-markets' into many of the key services of the welfare state (particularly the health service, but now into social services) some might argue that this notion of the user as consumer is becoming more meaningful. However, the 'consumers' of health and social services are still in a very different position from consumers in the market place, and therefore the notion of consumer choice is misleading. Despite the introduction of internal markets, it is still not the user as such who is the 'purchaser'. It is usually the doctor or the social worker (or 'care manager') who actually buys the services on behalf of the patient or user, and it is not just the interests and needs of that user that are taken into account, but also the level of resources available in the budget and the agreements the purchaser may have to contract with certain providers. Although users may have more choice than previously, it is still restricted. Of course, the notion that consumers in a market place can exercise free choice is not true. The extent to which choice can be exercised depends upon the wealth and the power of the consumers. Berry has argued that the perspective which sees consumerism as about offering choice is interpreted as letting market forces have a controlling influence:

> This moves away from the idea of universal entitlement to benefit or service towards a perception of the tenant or client as customer. It is a short step from here to introducing charges for services and basing choice on ability to pay. Since the ability to be perceived as a consumer is limited to those who can pay for the privilege, this analysis can also lead to the targetting of specific (second-class) programmes at those who are too poor to exercise that choice, too poor to be customers, or even to pay indirectly as tax- or ratepayers (Berry 1988, pp. 268–9).

According to Taylor, the so-called 'Citizen's Charter' produced by the British Government is in effect a consumers' charter in which choice means 'the right of exit from services starved of resources and left to wither' (Taylor 1991/2, p. 88). In fact, many users of social work services cannot be regarded as consumers even in the very tenuous sense we have discussed above. Some people, such as users of the probation service on a compulsory court order or a parent whose child is suspected of having been abused, do not have the right of exit from the 'service' – or if they do exit, their choice may be imprisonment, a fine, or removal of a child. This is does not mean that many of the users' rights promoted under the auspices of the new consumerism do not apply in the case of compulsory statutory social work involvement (such as rights to access to files, to information about legal rights). Indeed, many of them are now enshrined in the law. Rather, the idea of consumer *choice* makes even less sense in this context.

In some ways, the notion of the user as a consumer is quite a helpful one, provided it is not linked with the idea of consumer choice. It is more honest about the nature of the social work relationship, which is not a relationship between two free individual persons, or even two fellow citizens, but between representatives of an agency which provides or purchases services on behalf of the state and someone who enters into a relationship with that agency or its representatives for a specific purpose. While this may not be how social workers wish to see the relationship, this is, in effect, how it is, especially in the context of the statutory and purchasing side of local authority social services or the probation service.

New professionalism or new consumerism?

The increasing concern with users' rights has been termed both 'the new professionalism' and the 'new consumerism' in the social work literature. While the use of terminology may not always be significant, the two phrases do have different connotations. Significantly it is the professional association, BASW, which particularly uses the term 'new professionalism'. In the introduction to its model complaints procedure, the following statement is made:

> The new professionalism, of which BASW has been in the vanguard, is committed to shifting the balance of power between the worker and client by consolidating the rights of the client, by securing client participation in decision-making, and by opening up services to consumer influence. Complaints procedures, so often seen as a threat by social workers, have a vital part to play in helping to change the

organisational culture of social work agencies. They safeguard and secure clients' rights. They provide a foundation for good professional practice based on respect for clients as equal citizens. And they provide a useful mechanism to monitor how agencies are viewed by recipients of their services (BASW 1989, p. iii).

BASW states that the new approach to professionalism does not draw upon the traditional models of medicine and law (presumably meaning the model of professional as expert), but incorporates ideas of participation and rights derived from the consumer movement. It is suggested that BASW has taken a leading role in developing this new approach since publishing 'Clients Are Fellow Citizens' in 1980. Although the quotation from BASW given above seems to elide the notions of citizen and consumer, as do several other commentators (for example, Bamford 1990, p. 57) arguably the new professionalism (as opposed to the new consumerism) is about users as fellow citizens.

The new professionalism is about giving more power to users in the context of the professional relationship, but the focus is on the professional as the one giving the power. So although the user may be given more rights, it could be argued that it is still the professional that is in control. The new consumerism, on the other hand, is moving away from the idea of the social worker as a professional who exercises professional judgement on the basis of expertise, towards the idea of social workers as officials – as distributers of resources according to certain prescribed standards and procedures. The new consumerism, in that it emanates both from the Conservative government and from the consumer rights movement, has strong strands of anti-professionalism embedded in it, exemplifying a desire to challenge the power and exclusiveness of professional groups (in medicine, law, and education, as well as social work). The new professionalism may be trying to hang on to some of the status and power, or at least the identity, of the professional, while also becoming more responsive to user rights – developing a new model of professionalism which does not have to be elitist and exclusive. As Bamford says: 'The new professionalism does not deny the existence of that [professional] knowledge and skill but seeks to bridge the gap between worker and client, and to widen the range of choices open to the client' (Bamford 1990, p. 57).

The new professionalism seeks to retain the notion of the social worker as a professional requiring special education and adhering to a professional code of ethics while trying to regard the user as more of an active participant. The traditional values still apply, although the way they are put into practice has changed. For example, promoting user self-determination is now extended to include user participation in decision-making. In practice it is difficult to separate out the new professionalism and the new consumerism. Developments which began as part of the new professionalism (for example, complaints procedures, advocacy and contracts between worker and user) have become absorbed into the broader changes brought about by government legislation and the new consumerism. The new consumerism tends to see the social worker more as a provider of services (which would include assessment and care planning) according to certain standards and criteria. Some of the traditional values still seem relevant. For example, user self-determination means users having the choice whether to accept the service or not, or whether to complain. The social worker has to individualise the service (which relates to treating each person as a unique individual) to take account of individual needs. However, this must be according to the criteria laid down and the type of needs prioritised by the agency, so the social worker becomes more of a rule-follower and the principles of fairness and consistency in allocating resources will be important.

The next half of this chapter will consider some of the recent developments associated with the new consumerism/professionalism relevant to enhancing users' rights. We will consider whether the gap between day to day social work practice and the general principles relating to user self-determination in the codes of ethics can be bridged by national or agency codes of practice in matters such as access to records, complaints procedures and user participation.

Access to records, complaints and user participation

Recent legislation and policy guidance in the late 1980s and early 1990s has required social services departments to give users the right to see the information kept in their personal files, to make complaints about standards of services, and has encouraged the participation of users in decision-making about their cases. This is obviously a very important way in which users can be given more power in the social work relationship and treated with respect. Newcastle City Council's policy statement on access to information (Newcastle upon Tyne Social Services Department no date) includes the following principle: 'Underlying this policy statement is the principle that it is unethical and ineffective to be working with people without sharing fully objectives, plans and information on which these are based.'

Shared recording and open access to records are said to enhance users' rights and therefore give them more power in the social work process (BASW 1983). This can be further strengthened by the use of explicit contracts or agreements between users and social workers (Corden and Preston-Shoot 1987). Some commentators, however, question to what extent this is the case (Payne 1989; Rojeck and Collins 1987; 1988). Although shared recordings and contracts do encourage more honesty between the social worker and the user, they do not necessarily enhance the user's freedom in a positive sense, unless they are also accompanied by a commitment on the part of the social workers to supporting users to participate in decision-making. Further, the records are still kept by the social services departments and although users have a right to see them, this is often treated as a concession. According to the organisation PAIN (Parents Against Injustice) quoted in Chamberlain (1992, p. 14), parents who believe they have been wrongly accused of child abuse face great difficulties if they ask to see their files. In addition, many of the procedures are quite time-consuming and cumbersome. A typical procedure for dealing with users' requests to see their files, for example, involves forms being completed, and then a responsible officer tracing the information requested which may be located on computer and in manual files in several different sections. Letters must be sent out to third parties and health professionals and the information will need to be collated and possibly edited. The applicant must be given help by means of explanation and interpretation to understand the information. In some cases preparatory counselling may be needed (for example where someone looks at the records concerning their adoption) and there must also be procedures for the user to challenge and change the record and to appeal if access is denied.

Similar blocks also occur for users wishing to make complaints. Even if leaflets are produced outlining the range of services available, the standards of treatment to be expected and outlining how to make complaints, social work users are very often reluctant to complain. A report on residential homes for older people suggests that older people in care are often afraid to complain because they think it would be useless and dangerous. They have very little access to the outside world and are totally in the control of the people running the home (Counsel and Care 1992). A recent report from the National Consumer Council (1993) found that people felt grateful for social services and guilty about complaining. As one person commented 'the sense that we do not have a right to service raises fears that we will lose what we have got, as a punishment for making a fuss'. This tends to suggest that the publication of a leaflet saying people can complain is not enough to create a climate where users feel they have a right to social services. Some users may need an advocate to speak on their behalf. The kind of climate that would make it easier for users who are regular users of a service to complain might be created if user involvement in service planning and delivery has been encouraged and social workers or others have spent some time working with the users to develop their skills and confidence. This kind of work is only possible if the workers are in regular contact with the users, or if the users are part of a self-help or campaigning group or seek the assistance of an advocacy project.

Procedures have been developed within the community care assessment process for users' own definition of their problems and their needs to be recorded and taken into account. Similarly within procedures for assessing risk to children and their needs for care, the views of the child should be sought and taken into account, as should those of the parents. Many local authorities, for example, have policies and procedures encouraging parents to attend initial child protection case conferences where decisions about their children are to be made, although this is not a legal right. Similar shortcomings in implementing these procedures exist as for the others discussed above. If parents are simply informed that they may attend a case conference, but not given any information about what to expect and no support in making their contribution, then the 'participation' may be nothing more than a token gesture. Recent research on parent participation in case conferences suggests that this is generally welcomed by all participants and most professionals think it improves the quality of the decisions made. However, Bell and Sinclair (1993, p. 25) conclude as a result of their study of parental involvement in initial case conferences in Leeds that:

> one of the unforeseen and unfortunate consequences of the professional's quite proper preoccupation with getting parental participation at case conferences right is a concentration on procedure and interagency communication at the expense of engagement with the child.

This raises again the issue of the 'proceduralisation' of child protection work and indeed of social work generally. It indicates that while procedures are necessary to ensure that the interests and rights of the child and the parents are all considered and decisions are taken according to relevant evidence in a fair manner, correctly following a mass of complex and time-consuming procedures can become the goal or end of the case conference rather than a means to achieving a fair decision.

The involvement of young people (and their parents) in case reviews raises similar problems. The degree of users' involvement or participation in decisions about their own cases obviously varies not just according to the policies of particular agencies and the commitment of individual social workers, but also according to the social worker's judgement regarding users' abilities to understand the situation and to make an informed statement of their own needs and choice of services or courses of action. This is why it may be appropriate for some users to have independent advocates to support them in speaking for themselves or to speak on their behalf. This is especially important where the social worker's role is to act on behalf of the agency in distributing resources or exercising control. In the new community care procedures, the worker (care manager) who assesses the user and purchases and manages the care package is separate from the person or organisation that provides the care. It might therefore be assumed that the care manager would advocate on behalf of the user to gain the best possible package. However, since the resources for purchasing are limited, and the social services department will have set some limits on certain types of services and prioritised the meeting of certain kinds of needs, the care manager will be constrained. The care manager may be working on behalf of the user, but he or she is also working for an agency. The rights and needs of the individual user will often conflict with agency policies for distributing available resources between users; and needs that cannot be met may not be taken into account.

This discussion of access to records, complaints procedures and participation in decision-making suggests that laws, policies and procedures can lay the ground rules for users' rights, but are meaningless if not developed alongside the commitment of agencies and workers to give support and resources for users to exercise their rights. In the next part of this chapter we will look at various ways of doing this, including the promotion of advocacy, user involvement, and empowerment.

Advocacy

In recent years there has been a growth in advocacy projects in Britain. This trend has been reinforced by the National Health

Service and Community Care Act 1990 which requires wide consultation of users in the drafting of community care plans and in the process of assessment. The Disabled Persons Act 1986 provides for the appointment of a representative or advocate for the disabled person to act on their behalf in connection with the provision of social services. Although the relevant sections of the Act (1, 2 and 3) have never been implemented (Vernon 1993, p. 118), the concept of advocacy is being taken on board by many social services departments and voluntary sector agencies. In County Durham, for example, an Advocacy Project was established in 1992 (Durham County Advocacy Project 1993), with the aim of promoting a range of types of advocacy. Different kinds of advocacy include: citizen advocacy which gives training to volunteers to work with service users on a long-term one to one basis; professional advocacy which tends to involve a more short-term relationship in which an advocate with special knowledge or skills helps the user with particular decisions; and self-advocacy which involves training users to develop the skills and confidence to speak up for themselves (*Newcastle upon Tyne Community Care Plan* 1993, p. 99). Advocacy is based on the notion of enabling users to articulate their needs and ensuring that their rights are respected. When users are unable to speak for themselves and do not have the capacity to decide what type of needs they have or how they would like them to be met, then the advocate will have to act in what is judged to be their best interests.

Advice, Advocacy and Representation Services for Children (ASC) is a project set up in 1992 designed to help young people who feel their voices are not being heard (Dalrymple 1993). The Director comments that it has been hard to convince those responsible for caring for young people of the importance of advocacy services. When schemes have been set up for ASC representatives to visit a residential home on a regular basis to offer a confidential and independent service to young people, this can seem threatening to some staff. She reports that: 'Our experience is that staff (both field and residential) who support the service and actively promote it to young people are those who are also committed to respecting young people with whom they are working' (Dalrymple 1993, p. 13).

User involvement

User involvement in planning and delivering services is another important aspect of the community care legislation. The promotion of user involvement became popular in the 1980s and has been partly linked to a general trend in local authorities to 'democratise' their services – which includes bringing them closer to people (decentralising offices), making them more responsive to local needs (through consulting and perhaps involving local people in local community councils or neighbourhood forums), and developing systems to promote the participation of local people and service users in the planning and delivery of services. In a social services context these moves have often been linked with the development of 'patch' based offices and 'community social work' (Hadley and McGrath 1980; 1984; Beresford 1984). Bayley sees such locally based work as coming about because of the recognition that the community itself is the main provider of care, and that formal services must be organised to fit in with informal caring networks (Bayley 1989, p. 45). This is obviously one very important reason in terms of effectiveness of services; other reasons might include concerns around reducing the distance between the user and the worker (as expert professional), seeing individual users' problems as problems shared with other local people, and developing community action as well as community care systems.

There is an important difference between decentralising service delivery (for example, moving social workers from a city centre office to neighbourhood-based offices in a small patch) and democratising services (encouraging participation and sharing power with local people and users). The former may fit in well with viewing the user as a relatively passive consumer (with the main concern being to meet her or his needs as effectively as possible) and the latter with the user as an active citizen with a right to have a say in and some control over how services are planned and delivered. The move to genuine participation of local people in service delivery and policy making, which would involve politicians and officials sharing some of their power with local people, is less easy to achieve and less common than approaches which inform, consult or merely involve local people or users. As Croft and Beresford (1989, p. 107) comment, neither of the two best known patch social services projects (Dinnington and Normanton) were able to indicate any significant transfer of say and control to service users or local people. This is partly because of reluctance to give up power, but also because of the time and effort needed to support and train users to participate effectively and above all the difficulty of encouraging local people or users to want to participate. Those who do participate may be a few experienced activists, whose opinions cannot be assumed to represent those of other local people or users. This type of participation may be no more than a token gesture towards genuine participatory democracy. Walzer speaks of 'the sharing of power amongst the activists ... the rule of the people with most evenings to spare' (quoted in Gyford 1991, p. 179).

Bearing this in mind, the skills, approaches and values of those social workers who do attempt to promote more than token user involvement tend to be of the more 'radical' kind, closer to those of community workers, with an emphasis on skills in mobilising and empowering individuals to work together collectively, seeing problems experienced as part of wider social and economic conditions, and working to change the attitudes and policies of agencies, councillors and society in general. The time needed for this kind of developmental work is considerable, and unless a social worker has a brief to work directly with groups or communities, then it is unlikely that he or she will find the time to develop such approaches. Croft and Beresford (1989, p. 107) quote a comment from a worker on a patch project: 'It is difficult to make space to develop innovatory approaches given continuing statutory responsibilities, particularly when the team is not fully staffed.'

It is easier for community workers or group workers who have a specific brief to do this kind of work, and whose skills and values are less oriented to the individual user, to develop styles of working that focus on 'empowering' users, groups and communities.

Empowerment

'Empowerment' is another contested concept which it is important to mention in this context. Rather like user involvement, it has a range of meanings from giving users some limited choices (the consumerist approach) to power sharing (the citizenship approach) to supporting and encouraging people or groups to realise their own power and take action for themselves (a 'radical' approach). A 'radical' approach is often advocated through linking empowerment to oppression, and seeing empowerment as part of anti-oppressive practice (see for example, Ahmad 1990; Mullender and Ward 1991; Thompson 1993). Thompson defines oppression as:

> Inhuman or degrading treatment of individuals or groups; hardship and injustice brought about by the dominance of one group over another; the negative and demeaning exercise of power. Oppression often involves disregarding the rights of an individual or group and thus is a denial of citizenship (Thompson 1993, p. 31).

The rhetoric of anti-oppressive practice is generally couched in terms of challenging structural oppression – that is, challenging the systems of beliefs, policies, institutions and culture that systematically discriminate against and demean women, Black people, differently abled people, lesbians and gays, working class people and other oppressed groups. Yet as this rhetoric is incorporated into mainstream practice (as it now is in Britain) it is questionable sometimes whether 'empowerment' and 'anti-oppressive practice' consist of anything more than enabling individual users to gain confidence and offering 'individually sensitive practice' that takes account of, for example, a user's dietary and religious needs and their personal experience of oppression. This is not to undermine some of the radical and challenging work that has happened and is taking place, but rather to suggest that this does not represent the mainstream of social work practice, despite the lip-service that is paid to anti-oppressive work. As we commented in chapter 2, the values relating to challenging structural oppression are in fundamental opposition to the individualistic values underpinning traditional social work.

Mullender and Ward in their book *Self-Directed Groupwork: Users Take Action for Empowerment* (1991) produce a statement of values or practice principles for empowering practice. This is a good example of some of the principles being promoted by the 'new professionalism' regarding non-elitism and the participation of users in defining the agenda to be worked on. Yet it adds to these by adopting a structural approach to the cause of social problems and advocates challenging structural oppression while at the same time maintaining the traditional individualistic values of respect for persons and the right to self-determination. While the examples given in the book are very varied and include some that were campaigning for change, the title of the book might suggest the focus is on empowerment as an end in itself ('users take action for empowerment') rather then a means to an end (which might be 'users become empowered to take action for change'). Obviously the process is circular and it is impossible to separate out empowerment from action (see the discussion in chapter 3 relating to 'praxis' and the work of Freire). But in social work generally the emphasis is more on individual users becoming more confident and personally powerful, rather than achieving societal change. Thompson's definition tends to reflect this when he states that empowerment: 'involves seeking to maximise the power of clients and to give them as much control as possible over their circumstances. It is the opposite of creating dependency and subjecting clients to agency power' (Thompson 1993, p. 80).

In talking of users gaining control over rather than changing their circumstances, this suggests that the aim is to empower people to live a better quality of life in the world as it is. Of course, other parts of Thompson's book on anti-discriminatory practice do embrace societal change, but the focus in social work generally is on the individual user or family and therefore inevitably the stress is on personal change, even if the broader societal context is acknowledged. This is particularly evident in the literature related to the development of community care and the promotion of the rights of people with disablties (see Ramon 1991). Whilst the existence of structural oppression is frequently acknowledged and the role of social workers in challenging it is emphasised, in practice much of the work they do is about helping people with disabilities 'conform' to what is accepted as 'normal' behaviour (for a critique of normalisation theory see Dalley 1992; Brown and Smith 1992).

Conclusions

In this chapter we have examined the gradual shift from seeing the user as a person, to user as fellow citizen, to user as consumer. In one sense the move towards a consumer rights approach can be regarded as a development of the principle of respect for persons, in that it is actualising the rights of a person in the specific situation of being a social work user – in particular, rights to information, certain standards of service and to choice. We noted the recent development of codes of practice and procedures for gaining access to records, shared record-making, shared decision-making and making complaints. Within the predefined boundaries of the social work relationship and the agency context, these procedures aim to give users more power. But the procedures in themselves do not guarantee respect for the user as an equal citizen or a consumer with real choice; the social worker, for example, will generally be more powerful and articulate than the user and there may be constraints in terms of agency resources. These procedures need to be developed alongside a systematic and long term approach which promotes the participation of users in service delivery, works towards empowerment and offers advocacy for those users who find it difficult to articulate their needs and rights. This is not an easy task, as it is time-consuming and involves social workers and agencies being prepared to give up some of their power and change their ways of working. It also brings into focus the contradictions between individual and structural approaches to change. While social workers may work towards empowering individuals to take control over parts of their personal lives, unless the policies and practices in the welfare state and in society generally which oppress certain individuals and groups are changed, then social work can only go so far towards putting these principles into action.

Exercise 3

Aims of the exercise – to encourage the reader to think practically about what rights are possible and desirable in relation to a context of which he/she has experience.

1. Think of an agency that you are currently working for/have worked for.
2. Draw up a list of what you think should be the users' rights in relation to their contact with this agency.
3. Why do you think these particular rights are important?
4. How would you ensure that they are put into practice?

6

Social Workers' Duties: Policies, Procedures and the New Managerialism

In the last chapter we focussed on users' rights. According to our definition of a right, if users have certain rights, then some person or some institution has a corresponding duty to fulfil those rights. In many cases it may be the social worker directly (for example, the duty to treat the user with respect), or it may be the social worker indirectly acting on behalf of an agency (the duty to provide services for children in need). The direct duties could be said to be inherent in the role of professional social worker, and the indirect ones inherent in the particular job the social worker has. In this chapter we will explore what is the nature of social workers' duties to users in relation to their other duties including those to the employing agency, to the profession and to society. The professional codes have most to say about duties to users and to the profession and tend to argue that these duties have primacy. Agencies, on the other hand, tend to require that employees put agency policies and procedures first. This chapter will explore the conflicts that arise between different sets of duties, particularly in the context of the increasing proceduralisation and bureaucratisation of social work ('the new managerialism').

Duties

The types of duties we have been talking about (those to the profession and to the employing agency) are those that people

118

commit themselves to when they take on the job of social worker. In this sense, a duty is a consequence of a contract or undertaking, either implicit or explicit: 'My duty is that which I am engaged or committed to do, and which other people can therefore expect and require me to do. I have a duty to keep a promise, because I have bound myself thereto' (Whitley 1969, p. 54).

However, we may have conflicting duties, because different commitments may have been undertaken which are incompatible with each other in a particular situation. Therefore, we may have to choose between different duties. For example, I have a duty to keep the information users give me confidential; but I also have a duty to protect users from serious danger. Therefore I might decide to break the confidence of a young person who has said she is planning to commit suicide. The duty of confidentiality may be said to be a 'prima facie' duty – that is, it is what I ought to do, other things being equal. This notion of duty is connected also with accountability; if I have made a contract or undertaking to do something (duty) then I am also expected to be able to explain or justify my performance or nonperformance of that duty (accountability). In social work this latter aspect of a duty is regarded as important, as social workers must be publicly accountable for what they do.

It is important to distinguish this sense of duty – an obligation or commitment as a consequence of a contract or undertaking – from how the term is sometimes used, particularly in moral philosophy, to mean 'the right action'; 'what I ought to do'. We might say in relation to the above case, that I decided it was my duty to tell the girl's parents of her intention to commit suicide. 'Duty' in this sense is a definitive recommendation regarding what ought to be done taking all the circumstances into account. 'Duty' in this sense means *the* right action, and there is only one right action. Therefore it would not make sense to talk of a conflict of duties. I am going to use the term duty in the first sense, where duties are regarded as commitments or obligations which may be in conflict with each other. Therefore a duty is what I am committed to do, other things being equal. Very often, other things are not equal. It may be morally right for me to neglect one particular duty in favour of another. When talking about duty in the sense of the right action, or what I ought to do having taken all circumstances into account, I will use terms like 'making a moral judgement about how to act' or 'deciding on the morally right course of action'.

Social work as a 'role-job'

Social work takes place within an institutional framework of rights and duties defined by the law, the employing agency and the professional code. Chapter 4 discussed the duties of the social worker as laid down in the professional code of ethics. There are other rights and duties which make up the job, such as the legal right (or power) and/or the duty to intervene in people's lives in cases where a child is thought to be at risk, or the procedural duty to follow agency procedures in assessing risk in child protection cases. For this reason Downie and Loudfoot (1978) describe social work as a 'role-job' – meaning that the job of social work is defined by a set of institutional rights and duties. They argue that it is important for social work to have an institutional framework because social workers intervene in the lives of others and it is in the interests of users that they have a right to intervene. Secondly, social workers discover many intimate details of people's lives and it is important that there are rules, such as confidentiality, which provide security for the user. Thirdly, social workers themselves can find security from working in an institutional framework – for example they can fall back on their official position to give guidance on proper procedures with a user in case of legal action.

Downie and Loudfoot list four different types of rights and duties that attach to the role of social worker, to which I have added a fifth:

1. Legal rights and duties to users, employers and others.
2. Professional rights and duties arising from membership of a profession with its own standards of conduct.

3. Moral duties arising from the fact that the social worker is dealing with specific individuals in specific situations.
4. Social duties arising from the fact that the social worker is also a citizen who has the opportunity to do more civil good than many; for example, through working towards reforming or changing social policies.
5. Procedural rights and duties arising from the fact that the social worker is employed by an agency which has its own rules concerning how the work should be done and how social workers should behave.

When someone takes on the job of a social worker, they are in effect agreeing to work within this framework of rights, duties and rules. In particular, the employing agency will expect them to work within its rules and procedures, since it is this agency that is paying their wages. Usually an employing agency will also expect the worker to work within the framework of the law and indeed if it is a statutory agency many of its policies and procedures will be based on interpretations of Acts of Parliament and Statutory Guidance.

Conflicting duties

In an ideal world it might be assumed that legal, professional, social and moral rights and duties would complement or coincide with those required by the agency. However, this is not always the case. A social worker may judge that the employing agency's procedures regarding confidentiality are too lax compared with the standards laid down in the professional code, for example, or that the methods it uses entail treating users as objects rather than respecting them as persons. The professional associations usually state that it is the principles laid down in the professional codes that should come first as these codes are designed with the protection of users in mind, whereas the law or agency rules may be designed for the convenience of the majority.

In taking on the role of social worker a person takes on several different layers of duties which may conflict with each other. We can summarise these duties and the main sources of guidance as follows:

1. **Duties to users** – for example, to respect users' rights to make their own decisions, to respect their rights to confidentiality, to safeguard and promote the welfare of children (acting on behalf of the local authority). Sources of guidance include the professional code of ethics; agency policies and codes of practice; the law; public opinion; charters for users' rights.
2. **Duties to the profession** – for example, to uphold the good name of social work by maintaining effective and ethical practice. Sources of guidance include: the professional code of ethics; guidance from the professional association.
3. **Duties to the agency** – for example, following the prescribed rules and procedures, safeguarding the reputation of the agency. Sources of guidance include: the worker's job description and contract; agency policies and procedures.
4. **Duties to society** – for example, maintaining social order, executing the responsibilities of local authority social services departments, or probation services as laid down by statute. Sources of guidance include: the law; government guidance; public opinion.

How does the social worker judge between these different duties when they conflict? The professional code aims to cover all these areas and suggests that its guidance should come first in cases of conflict. This implies that first and foremost a social worker is a professional, and it is from this stance that all other duties must be judged. For example, if the agency policies and procedures contravene the ethical principles stated in the code, then the social worker must not collude with this, and must try to change them. Yet there are also cases where different obligations in the code itself conflict – such as the duties to maintain confidentiality and to promote user welfare. How do we resolve these? Surely it is the *person* in the role of professional who has to decide which duties have priority – not only within the code, but between different sets of duties to the agency and to society? Ultimately it is a person's own personal moral code that will determine what action is morally right.

The relationship between personal, professional and agency values

The tendency of some of the professional codes (particularly the Swedish one as was noted in chapter 4) to suggest that social work is a vocation, and that it involves taking on certain duties in one's personal life, can lead to a blurring of the distinction between the personal and the professional. It is as if the person becomes a social worker as part of their personal identity, and the duties attaching to being a social worker are the same as, or become the same as, personal or private rights and duties. This type of view might be akin to someone taking on a religious calling – becoming a priest/priestess – whose whole life should be lived according to the moral duties of the religion, not just parts of it when he or she is performing the role of a priest/priestess. This is the kind of view taken by Wilkes (1985, p. 54) who notes Lewis and Maude's three views of professionals: as tradespeople with special skills; as officials using their techniques to modify people's conduct; or as:

> guardians of a tradition, humane and Christian, of study and service to their fellows, whether this is based on a confidential and fiduciary relationship with individual clients or on voluntary sacrifice of extra monetary gain in the interests of the community (Lewis and Maude, quoted in Wilkes 1985, p. 54).

Wilkes argues for this latter view of the professional social worker. This may seem a strange attitude to have towards state-sponsored social work in the late-twentieth century. However, it may be easier to understand if we look more carefully at the professional code and note that the kinds of duties it espouses are those of the liberal individualist ethics that are current in western society generally. The Swedish Code, the International

Code and some of the others are based on the United Nations Declaration of Human Rights. They are advocating the kind of moral behaviour that it is thought any morally upright decent human being should follow. This is why Ronnby (1993) asks why social workers feel the need to add in writing to their professional codes that one shall respect every human being's unique worth and integrity: 'Social worker's ethics do not differ from those that characterise others' humanistic ideals'. In effect, he is saying that there should be no need for a code of ethics for social work, because the person who is a social worker should have their own personal ethical code which involves treating others with respect as fellow human beings. According to Ronnby (1993, pp. 5–6):

> The prerequisite of ethically proper actions in social work would be that the social worker cares about, even cares for, the help seeker. The social worker must dare, and be able, to open herself for the client; she must be capable of being herself with open senses, feelings and empathy. Techniques and routines as well as professional self-interest can prevent the social worker from acting humanely.

This seems to amount to an argument against the separation of the personal and the professional. It may not amount to an argument against the notion that social work is a role-job with specific rights and duties attached to it; but it does imply that the specific rights and duties should not be fundamentally different from or in opposition to the general moral principles by which the social worker leads her life. Ronnby notes the tendency for the welfare state (of which social work is a part) to reinforce existing inequalities in society and to treat those who are the poorest and least powerful as objects to be pitied or changed. His solution is for social workers to adhere to their personal humanistic ethics and to come closer to their users as fellow human beings. A similar view is argued for by Halmos (1978) and Wilkes (1981). In Table 6.1 I have called this kind of model that of the social worker as a committed practitioner, who regards her work as a way of putting into practice her personal moral values.

But the view that the social worker should genuinely care about her users and treat them as she would friends or strangers in her ordinary life seems problematic in the context of current social work practice. Whilst out shopping on a Saturday I might give £10 out of my pocket to a man in the street who asked for some money for food, and take him home for a cup of coffee. But surely I should not give £10 out of my pocket to a social work user in the office who asked for money for food and take him home for a cup of coffee whilst on duty as a social worker on Monday? First, this might leave me open to accusations of favouritism, as I cannot do this with all users. Secondly, if I did give this level of personal care to all users I would be impoverished and exhausted. Thirdly, this would involve developing a personal relationship with a user which might leave him and me open to abuse. These reasons echo those given by Downie and Loudfoot as to why it is important that social work operates within an institutional framework of rights and duties; to protect both the social worker and the user. It is doubtful if Halmos, Wilkes or Ronnby are actually arguing that social workers should treat users as friends. Rather that we should treat them as fellow human beings for whom we feel empathy and respect, and that we should regard ourselves as people first and social workers second, applying the same fundamental ethical principles to the situations we encounter in social work as we would to other situations in other parts of our lives. However, as social workers we are employed by an organisation which operates by certain rules and procedures and we are constrained by societal mores and the legal system. Within this framework we should treat users with as much honesty and respect as possible, but it is not part of the job to care for our users unconditionally. It is arguably more important that the social worker holds on to her own personal values not in order to give unconditional love to users, but in order to challenge laws, policies and practices regarded as unjust. This point relates to another model of social work practice which I have called the 'radical' in Table 6.1. While in some respects similar to the committed practitioner model in that it asserts that social work should be about putting into practice one's personal values, in this case it is more a question of political ideology and a commitment to working for social change. This kind of position was espoused by Marxists such as Corrigan and Leonard, or might be argued for by feminists and anti-racists (see chapter 2).

At the other extreme, Leighton argues for the separation of personal, professional and agency values. He suggests that social work aims to manipulate and change people; social workers act not as ordinary human beings as they would in their personal lives, but take on a separate role, which requires them to appear to care, but not in a genuine way that one would care for a friend. He gives the example of a social worker who needs to get certain intimate information from a young person in residential care (presumably for a report):

> The social worker is therefore obliged to try to draw the child into a relationship for no other purpose than to satisfy the social worker's job requirements. It is exceptional if the worker offers important parts of himself or herself to the child's personal social world. The relationship is part of a statutory and financial transaction from which only the social worker benefits financially (Leighton 1985, p. 78).

He argues that we must separate the personal and the professional, so that we do not feel guilty about manipulating people and using relationships as we would if we treated someone in the same way in ordinary life. According to Leighton, the social worker is required to:

> manipulate people and their relationships, and must learn the art of appearing to care when his natural feeling is not to care. To survive as a private person and to do his work well he must sometimes operate within a mode of 'bad faith', a lack of absolute honesty in the relationship (Leighton 1985, p. 79).

Leighton's view seems rather extreme. It could ultimately lead to the social worker simply taking on a job and following all the procedures and practices required by the agency regardless of whether they appeared to be morally wrong according to the ethical principles of the profession or his or her own personal moral code. Taken to its limit, such a view could imply that the social worker working in a residential home where children were regularly tied to chairs and left without food could justify her or his actions by saying 'I was only doing my duty in accordance with the agency procedures' as if it was nothing to do with her or him if the agency procedures were immoral or cruel. This kind of response might emerge if the bureaucratic model outlined in Table 6.1 (page 129) was taken to its extreme and the social worker unquestioningly followed all agency rules and procedures.

This type of view seems to entail that there is no person over and above a series of social roles of which the private/personal is just one. Leighton gives an example of a social worker, Mr Anthony, and argues that certain values from his personal life, such as converting people to Catholicism and believing abortion to be morally wrong, conflict with professional values such as user self-determination and non-judgementalism, both of which conflict with employer's values such as assisting with birth control techniques and encouraging conformity to social norms. His conclusion seems to be that being a social worker is a totally different and separate thing from being a private individual. But is it? Surely the private individual or person decided to accept the job of social worker with its particular values and duties? If he was the kind of person who was such a strong Catholic that he went around trying to convert neighbours, friends and people in the street and he strongly opposed birth control, then arguably he would not have chosen to become a social worker. Most Catholics do not go around trying to convert people in the street or trying to dissuade strangers from having abortions. Surely the same moral standards Mr Anthony has for relating in his private life to strangers and acquaintances may apply also in social work? Or, rather, social work may be regarded as a particular setting in which certain ways of behaving are appropriate and to which particular duties apply. When Mr Anthony goes to a concert or visits the bank certain rules of behaviour apply which do not usually involve trying to convert the bank clerk or handing out anti-abortion leaflets in the concert hall. Leighton is right that the social worker should refrain from trying to persuade users not to have abortions and that social workers do not and cannot treat users as friends. However, he is mistaken in arguing that this means that personal, professional and agency values should be treated as totally separate. Where they conflict, the social worker as a person has a moral responsibility to decide which have primacy and to justify this decision. He may decide that he cannot work in an agency that involves so much work promoting birth control, or that he will request not to deal with certain cases where he would feel compromised. The diagram below illustrates the relationship between the personal, agency, professional and societal moral codes:

PERSON with own moral code	takes on role of	PROFESSIONAL SOCIAL WORKER with professional code of ethics	who takes	JOB OF SOCIAL WORKER in particular agency with specific responsibilities and duties

influenced and circumscribed by

SOCIETAL NORMS, PUBLIC OPINION, THE LAW

Professional, bureaucratic and committed/radical models of practice

Table 6.1 outlines three broad models of social work practice which I have called the professional, the bureaucratic and the committed/radical. As with all attempts at categorisation, this is obviously artifical, but it is a way of exploring the different emphases that social workers may adopt in their practice according to their ethical stance and according to the particular work setting in which they may be based. The professional model focusses on the social worker as an autonomous professional with expertise gained through education, and guidance coming from the professional code of ethics. Her first priority would be the rights and interests of users, and her identity as a social worker would be as a member of the profession first, and as a private individual or worker in an agency second. The bureaucratic model regards the social worker first and foremost as a worker in an agency with a duty to carry out the prescribed tasks and roles of that agency. Guidance comes from agency rules and procedures. The committed/radical practitioner model sees the social worker as a person who has chosen to take on the job out of a personal or ideological commitment to work for change and who puts this first. This model encompasses many different types of approach ranging

Table 6.1   *Models of social work practice*

	Professional	Bureaucratic	1 Committed/ 2 Radical
social worker as	professional	official/ technician	equal/ally
power from	professional expertise	organisational role	competence to deal with situation
service user as	client	consumer	equal/ally
focus on	individual worker– user relationship	service provision	1 Individual empowerment/ 2 Societal change
guidance from	professional code of ethics	agency rules and procedures	personal commitment/ ideology
key principles	users' rights to self-deter- mination, acceptance, confidentiality, etc.	agency duties to distribute resources fairly and to promote public good	1 empathy, genuineness 2 raising consciousness, collective action
organisational setting that would best facilitate this	private practice or large degree of autonomy in agency	bureaucratic agency in voluntary, statutory or private sector	independent voluntary agency or campaigning group.

from the individual 'ministration in love' model to the more collectivist approaches espoused by Marxists, feminists and anti-racists. Although the same heading has been used to encompass all these approaches, there are obvious differences in focus ranging from individual empowerment to societal change.

All three strands are evident in the social work literature and social work practice. The professional codes contain elements of all three, but the emphasis is more on the professional model, tempered with duties to the employing agency (bureaucratic) and personal commitment to work for societal change (committed/radical). Social work has never comfortably fitted into the role of 'professional expert' for reasons which include its ideological tendency to identify with the oppressed users and particularly its location in state-sponsored agencies. As Howe comments: 'I remain impressed with analyses which reveal social work to be largely a state-sponsored, agency-based, organisationally-tethered activity. It is not wise to tackle any examination of social work without taking note of this formidable context' (1991, p. 204).

This is why attempts to make social work fit into either the professional or the committed models are very difficult, given the organisational context. Indeed, at the present time the bureaucratic model is becoming more dominant, at least in the local authority sector and large voluntary organisations. However, with the increasing fragmentation of social work, and with services previously provided by social services departments being shifted to the private and voluntary sector, there is also an increasing opportunity in some areas of work for workers to operate within professional or committed models of practice. For example, specialist advocacy or counselling projects can be established with an unequivocal focus on the individual user–worker relationship, where it is very clear that the advocate or counsellor is primarily concerned with the rights or interests of the user. As it is increasingly recognised that people in powerless positions or who find it difficult to speak for themselves should have independent advocates to support them, then this is separating out the advocacy role from the general social work role. This means that the local authority social worker may be concerned with allocating and rationing resources between many users, whereas the adovcate will push for the wishes, needs and rights of this particular user.

So while it may often be the case that a social worker will find herself working within all three models (and hence experience conflicts of duties), the emphasis will vary not only according to the individual worker's view of her role, but also according to the particular piece of work being undertaken and the type of work setting. A social worker employed as a counsellor by an independent voluntary organisation to work in complete confidence with people with HIV/AIDS will find the organisational and work setting much more conducive to operating within a professional model of practice than a local authority-employed practitioner working in an Area Office as part of an Elderly Team, a large part of whose job is to assess and plan care packages for older service users. A community worker employed by a Tenants' Federation with a campaigning brief will find it easier to work within a radical model. If we look briefly at some of the key ethical principles for social work we can see how the organisational and work setting changes the interpretation and implementation of these principles.

1. **Confidentiality**

    HIV/AIDS counsellor – can assure complete confidentiality (privacy) between counsellor and user except in circumstances where it is legally permitted or required that the counsellor disclose information (e.g. where another is likely to be seriously harmed, or where a court requires information) (see Thomas et al., 1993; Bond, 1993).

    Social worker/care manager for the elderly – the limits of confidentiality are much broader and may include other members of the team, other health care professionals and service providers. If this particular social worker is unavailable or sick, then it would be expected that another social worker would consult the user's file and continue with the work. The relationship between user and worker is not a private one.

Community worker – while acknowledging the need to respect the confidentiality of certain personal information relating to individual tenants, confidentiality might be regarded as relatively unimportant in the context of tenants working together collectively to achieve change.

2. **The primacy of user self-determination and the user's interests**

HIV/AIDS Counsellor – while the counsellor may need to ration time between one user and another, and in exceptional cases consider the interests of others (e.g. if a user has not disclosed her/his HIV status to a partner), within these limits the counsellor can focus on the needs and interests of the user. It will depend on the style of the particular counsellor and the nature of the user's needs as to whether the counsellor respects the user's own choices and decisions or adopts a more parentalist or directive style.

Social worker/care manager for the elderly – this worker will need to keep in mind the needs and interests of other people as well as the user – for example, any family carers, neighbours, service providers and other current and potential users who will need resources. While the user's own choices and interests may be respected as far as possible, there are many limitations on this.

Community worker – would see promotion of individual self-determination or empowerment as part of the process of collective empowerment to achieve change

3. **Distributive justice**

HIV/AIDS counsellor – except, as we have mentioned, for the rationing of time between users, this worker does not have a direct role in distributing resources between individual users. The worker may choose to campaign and draw to the attention of service providers and policy makers the inadequacy of resources for this user group in particular and the discrimination they face in society; indeed the social work codes include this as a principle. It is interesting to note that this principle is not prominent in the code of ethics for counselling (British Association for Counselling 1992), which highlights a general difference in the roles of a counsellor (whose focus is primarily on helping the individual user) and the social worker (whose focus is the user in the context of a family, community or society).

Social worker/care manager for the elderly – this worker does have a duty to distribute the resources of the department fairly between individual users and to manage them efficiently. In making a decision about what course of action to take, resourcing issues will be as important as user choices and needs.

Community worker – will be concerned to achieve redistribution of resources (power, wealth, good housing) to tenants as a group according to need, linked to a striving for equality of result, and may use campaigning and community action approaches.

These examples suggest how the work setting – the type of agency and the role defined for the social worker – influence the extent to which a social worker may work more within one model than another. At the present time, as we have suggested, there is an increasing shift towards the bureaucratic model within statutory social work, which we will now explore.

The 'new managerialism' and the 'new authoritarianism'

In recent years there has been a growth in the production of procedural manuals in local authority social work. This is particularly noticeable in the field of child protection, although it is a trend throughout social work, and indeed the public, independent and private sector generally. This trend is related to the new consumerism and a concern to offer a consistent standard of service, linked to users' rights and quality assurance; the 'new managerialism' which seeks greater control over the work of employees; the 'new authoritarianism' which emphasises the social control function of practitioners; and a de-professionalising trend which seeks to see social workers as officials carrying out agency policy. In child protection, these trends have been given added impetus by the series of public inquiries in the 1980s into child abuse cases where either children died in their homes, or they were taken away from home unnecessarily and it was said that social workers should have acted differently. This has led to a vast quantity of guidance and advice from central government about how to assess children thought to be at risk, how to monitor them and their families, how to conduct inter-agency case conferences, how to investigate suspected cases of child abuse and how to prepare evidence for court (for example, Department of Health 1988). Most statutory agencies now have child protection manuals which contain this kind of information and give detailed guidance on the procedures that social workers should follow. Harris (1987) notes the tendency that this encourages towards defensive social work, whereby social workers 'go by the book' and are as concerned about protecting themselves and the agency as they are about the interests of the user. Howe (1992) talks of the 'bureaucratisation' of child care work, and McBeath and Webb (1990–1) note the technicist language of one of the key books of guidelines produced by the Department of Health (*Protecting Children* 1988). Cooper (1993, p. 45) warns that: 'Social workers who are simply agents of protection agencies may find it more difficult to operate beyond official procedures and guidelines arising from legislation, more difficult to use professional discretion in taking risks.'

If we take the example of child protection work, it could be argued that a new perspective is emerging. As Howe comments:

> injury and neglect suffered by some children results in the demand that children should be protected; that protection is achieved by improving, standardising and prescribing full and proper methods of investigation and assessment; and that bureaucratic forms of organisation appear to be the best way of handling the ever more detailed and complex requirements of this new perspective (Howe 1992, pp. 496–7).

King and Trowell (1992, p. 7) comment that social workers from both statutory and voluntary agencies: 'find themselves spending less time working to support and advise parents, and offering services to help needy children, and more time investigating allegations of child abuse, collecting evidence and helping bring cases before the courts'.

Parton argues that in a time of increasing public concern about child abuse and limited resources for social work, the aim of social work is to predict which families are 'dangerous' and therefore to protect children from abuse in these families by removing them (Parton and Small 1989; Parton 1989; 1991). The rest of the families who are not regarded as dangerous, should be left alone. The assumption is that there is a scientific method which can predict with relative accuracy the levels of risk that children may be subject to in their families and home environments. Most of the child protection manuals work on the basis of a checklist of predictors (for example, is there evidence of sustained, stable and sound family relationships; are there supportive networks; is the child generally well cared for?). However, the manuals do not suggest how each factor should be weighed against another, nor do they offer any statistical methods for calculating risk. This is because it would be a fairly meaningless exercise. Although it would be possible to ask social workers to place a numerical score against each predictor, and then to calculate an overall level of risk, would this actually help in predicting which children were most likely to be at risk of abuse? Parton (1989) quotes research using a checklist of predictors applied to the maternity notes of women discharged from a maternity unit. Of the families screened, 18% (511 out of 2802) were predicted as being 'at risk' of child abuse. Subsequently, 19 out of the 28 recognised cases were in this predicted high-risk group. So only nine cases were missed (false negatives). However, 492 were included in the original high-risk group that did not subsequently abuse (false positives). Parton concludes:

> We do not have the predictive tools to identify correctly all actual and potential cases of abuse – nor are we likely to have them. What,

therefore, is the balance to be struck between missing some (false negative) and falsely accusing others (false positive)? For efforts to keep false negatives to a minimum will increase the likelihood of false positives, while attempts to reduce false positives will increase the likelihood of tragedies in false negatives. While research can clarify such issues, how they are resolved is essentially a political and ethical question – in the same way as how child abuse is itself defined is essentially a political and ethical question (Parton 1989, p. 68).

To regard child protection purely as a technical exercise is misguided and ignores the ethical questions which are really about how much 'abuse' is society prepared to tolerate, balanced against how much interference in family life is thought to be justified. As was argued in chapter 1, social workers are faced with trying to balance these contradictory, ambivalent and changing societal values. Their major role becomes one of surveillance and collecting evidence, rather than therapy with the families. The function they are playing is more about social control than about care and therapy (Howe 1992).

Major changes in approach are also taking place in the field of community care, following the implementation of the National Health Service and Community Care Act in 1993 with its stress on assessment and care management. Detailed guidance from central government has been provided (Department of Health 1991a, 1991b), which has been developed into local authority manuals and procedures about how to conduct assessments, plan care packages, draw up contracts with providers of services and monitor standards and quality. Again, the language is largely technical and standardised forms are often used. Yet although the views of users and carers are to be taken into account, ultimately the decision regarding what services to provide and how will depend on availablity of resources and political and ethical decisions about priorities for types of user groups and services. Indeed the Department of Health guidance states:

> to ensure consistency of resource allocation between users with similar needs, authorities or agencies may wish to issue guidelines to their staff on the levels of expenditure appropriate to different needs. Some discretion will be necessary if flexible, individualised responses are to develop (1991a, p. 65).

The guide goes on to state that practitioners have to balance their accountability to users and to their employing agency. It recommends that users are informed of the ways of making representations under complaints procedures, if they are dissatisfied. It is acknowledged that practitioners will experience the stress of identifying needs for which no resources are available.

These changes in the field of child protection and community care represent major shifts in the role of social workers. We already noted the emphasis on users' rights, complaints, user involvement, starting from users' needs rather than available services and adopting multi-disciplinary approaches in chapter 5. Some commentators argue that this represents a shift in attitude and behaviour on the part of social workers and other professionals amounting to 'a cultural revolution' (Audit Commission 1992, p. 19). Yet in some ways such thinking is much less revolutionary for social workers than is being suggested. First, the values of social work have always been about 'putting the user first' and the current of 'anti-professionalism' within social work has always been strong. Secondly, despite the rhetoric about user-centred, needs-led services, in a time of resource shortage the reality is that economy and efficiency are often going to come before meeting the particular preferences and needs of users. The real revolution is arguably in the role that social workers are increasingly taking on as assessors, inspectors, gatherers of evidence and managers of budgets and in the fragmentation of the role of generic social worker into specialist functions with different titles. The duties required by the agency or employer are being defined in increasing detail. This leads at worst to defensive practice (going by the book and denying personal responsibility) and at best to bureaucratic practice (which focusses primarily on issues of resource allocation as determined by agency rules and procedures). Such an approach to practice can be distinguished from the 'professional' model which focusses more on the individual worker–user relationship with guidance from the code of ethics and the 'radical' or 'committed' model which stresses individual or societal change and does not separate out the personal from the professional or agency values (see Table 6.1).

While there is an increasing emphasis on the 'bureaucratic' model at the present time, there are constant tensions between all three and this is part of the reason why ethical dilemmas often arise in social work – because of the many layers of duties involved. We have already noted that much social work often takes place in bureaucratic settings where social workers may be taking on both 'professional' and 'official' roles; this tension between bureaucracy and professionalism was noted in chapter 4.

Ethics in bureaucracies: defensive versus reflective practice

Rhodes (1986, p. 134 ff) argues that bureaucratic decision-making undermines moral responsibility. She suggests that it is based on role and legal responsibility and encourages a split between personal and professional life – freeing employees from the demands of their personal moralities. For example, she says that:

> while you might *personally* wish to give welfare recipients more money, the organisation forbids it (p. 136).

> You may be urged to place a child in a foster home rather than a residential treatment school, because the more expensive treatment plan is viewed as 'inefficient' and 'costly' (p. 137).

She notes the contradictions between the individualised, caring concerns of social workers and the impersonal requirements of bureaucracies, and argues that 'being a good worker may mean acting unethically' (p. 137). However, we need to ask whether it is, in fact, unethical to refrain from giving welfare recipients more money? First, if it is just a question of me personally 'wishing' to do this, is it a moral judgement at all? If this were to be a moral judgement, it would be stated in terms of the fact that welfare recipients *ought* to have more money. If I make this moral judgement (accepting the position put forward in chapter 2 that moral judgements prescribe action and are universalisable), then it should commit me to action, and it would mean that other people in other areas in similar situations should be given more money. Yet if I give these people more money, others may have less; it may not be fair. If I break the rules for distributing money, then chaos will ensue. I could argue that it is in the greatest interest of the greatest number of people to stick to the rules at present because I am in an organisation that works by rules and is dealing with many people. If I decide to do this, surely I would not be acting 'unethically'? I would essentially be working from utilitarian moral principles relating to justice and fairness. It would be unethical if I *unthinkingly* always followed all agency rules and procedures; or if I *knowingly* acted unethically, using the agency rules as an excuse. There is a tendency to assume that questions around the distribution of resources, efficiency and cost are not ethical ones. They are, and it is dangerous not to regard them as such. Seeking the cheapest service may not be an unethical decision, if it can be argued that this results in more people getting some level of service, rather than a few people getting good quality service. It should be noted that Rhodes espouses a virtue-based ethical theory, which while consistent as a theory of ethics, does not reflect the system of morality currently predominant in social work (see chapter 2). Working in a bureaucracy does not inevitably mean acting 'unethically'; adopting utilitarian approaches is not necessarily unethical. In fact, it is vital to see such work as very much in the sphere of the ethical, rather than the purely technical. Otherwise there is the danger that we become 'defensive' practitioners. The ethical decisions regarding resource allocation or what is to count as child abuse may have been made elsewhere (by central government or by agency managers), but that does not absolve the social worker of the responsibility to challenge these decisions if necessary. For example, we need to guard against the preoccupation which the bureaucratic approach encourages with the distribution of existing resources, and think about arguing for more resources for social services users. The social worker in a bureaucracy can and should still be a 'reflective' practitioner. In summary, we may distinguish between defensive and reflective practitioners as follows:

- **Defensive practitioners** go by the book and fulfil duties/ responsibilities defined by the agency and the law. There is no need to take blame if the prescribed rules and procedures have been followed. Social workers are 'officials' or 'technicians'.

Doing 'my duty' means fulfilling my obligations to the agency, rather than doing the morally right action; personal and agency values tend to be separated, and the latter tend to be adopted whilst in the role of social worker.

- **Reflective practitioners** recognise ethical dilemmas and conflicts and how they arise (for example, through unequal power relationships with users; contradictions within the welfare state; society's ambivalence towards the welfare state and social workers in particular). They are more confident about their own values and how to put them into practice; they integrate knowledge, values and skills; reflect on practice and learn from it; are prepared to take risks and moral blame. There is a recognition that personal and agency values may conflict and that the worker as a person has moral responsibility to make decisions about these conflicts.

Conclusions

In this chapter we have discussed the many layers of often conflicting duties that social workers have to balance and choose between. We have argued that the critical or reflective practitioner needs to be aware of these and to make informed ethical judgements about which duties have priority. She may have to operate within several contradictory models of social work practice and be able to recognise and hold the tensions between them. If the social worker completely takes on one model to the exclusion of others, then important aspects of social work practice will be ignored. If the social worker regards herself exclusively as a 'professional', ignoring the constraints imposed by the employing agency, then she may become narrow and elitist. If she wholeheartedly takes on board the bureaucratic model she may become the defensive practitioner, mindlessly following agency rules. If she sees her own personal religious or political beliefs as paramount, then she may become unaccountable to her agency or to users. To recognise and balance these layers of duties is part of what it means to be a competent practitioner. We need to recognise that personal, professional, agency and societal values are interlocking, yet in tension.

Exercise 4

Aims of the exercise – to show how the values of the individual, the agency and society may be similar and/or conflicting.

1. Think of the job that you are currently doing, or one that you have done in the past:
   - What are your main *aims* in the job?
   - What *roles* do you play?
   - Describe your major *achievements* in this job.
   - What *values* do you think underpin your work in this job (what you regard as your major achievements may help you think through what your values are).
2. Now imagine looking at your job from the point of view of the agency you are working for or used to work for:
   - What do you think the agency's *aims* are?
   - What do you think is the agency view of the *role* you are playing?
   - What pieces of work do you think the agency would *value* most?
   - What *values* do you think underpin the agency's work?
3. Now imagine looking at your job from the point of view of society as a whole, or 'the public':
   - What do you think the public regards as the *aims* of the job?
   - What *role* do you think the public regards you as playing?
   - What pieces of work do you think the public would *value* most?
   - What *values* do you think underpin the public's view of your job?
4. Are there differences between your values and those of the agency and/or society? If so, why do you think this is the case?

7

Ethical Problems and Ethical Dilemmas in Practice

In this chapter we will look at some of the ethical problems and dilemmas that arise in everyday social work practice. Examples of problems and dilemmas have been collected from both trainee and experienced social workers, and will be explored in the light of the discussion in the previous chapters.

Developing the reflective practitioner: case studies from trainees

In discussing ethical dilemmas with trainee social workers, there is often an acute sense of confusion, anxiety and guilt around the decisions social workers have to make and the roles that they play. This may arise from a lack of understanding of the nature of the social worker's role (that it is complex and contradictory), idealism, a lack of information about policies and procedures, or simply a lack of opportunity to rehearse situations and learn from experience. An important part, therefore, of the education and training of social workers should be to facilitate the development of skills in critical reflection, which is where it is hoped this book will be helpful.

Developing a capacity for critical reflection is much more than simply learning procedures or achieving particular 'competences'. Part of the process of becoming a reflective practitioner is the adoption of a critical and informed stance towards practice. This can only come about through doing the practice, reflecting on it through dialogue and questioning, and changing the practice in the light of the reflection. This links to the concept of 'praxis' and the inseparability of theory and practice discussed in chapter 3. The notion of the helping professional as a reflective practitioner has been developed particularly by Schön (1983; 1987) and recently by Smith (1994) in the context of community educators. It is based on the notion of the practitioner reflecting on what is happening whilst in action, and reflecting on what happened afterwards ('reflection in and on action'). According to Brookfield: 'Practitioners develop strategies, techniques, and habitual responses to deal with different kinds of situations, drawing chiefly on their acquired experience and intuitive understanding' (Brookfield 1987, p. 156).

'Beginning' practitioners, or those with little experience, have obviously had less opportunity to gain experience and develop strategies and responses – or what Schön calls 'theories in use'. What a beginning practitioner may regard as an ethical dilemma – a choice between two equally unwelcome alternatives involving a conflict between ethical principles – an experienced practitioner may not. For the experienced practitioner it may be obvious that one alternative is less unwelcome than the other, or that one principle has priority over another, so she does not even conceptualise the decision as involving a moral dilemma. This does not mean that ethical issues are not involved, or that the situation should not be seen as involving an ethical problem, just that, strictly speaking, a dilemma is what confronts the worker before a decision is made. If the situation is familiar, or the worker has a clear sense of which moral principles have priority in this type of situation, then the situation will not be experienced as a dilemma, but simply a case of having to make a moral choice or decision. Thompson et al. (1988, pp. 2–3) distinguish between moral problems and moral dilemmas – arguing that a moral problem usually has a solution, or a possible solution. This seems to imply that a dilemma does not. However, I would argue that most of the time social workers do have to resolve dilemmas – in that they do have to take some action, even if this is deciding not to act, in which case they make a choice between the alternatives. This may be done either by making a random choice, or, more usually, after a process of reflection and research which eventually leads the worker to decide that one course of action may be better than another and therefore is the right action.

Some of the anxieties around the ethical dilemmas experienced by trainee social workers seem to be based on the following:

1. Lack of training and knowledge in a new situation.
2. Lack of clarity about the role of social worker, for example carer or controller, and rules attached to the role such as confidentiality.
3. Lack of confidence in their own status/position, especially vis-à-vis other professionals.
4. Narrow focus on the needs or rights of one individual user, or on one issue, without seeing the complexity of the case.
5. The complexity of the situation is seen, but found to be overwhelming.

The following cases from trainee social workers illustrate the above points. These are all examples of ethical dilemmas experienced by trainee social workers either whilst undertaking fieldwork practice, or before they joined a social work training programme (that is, when they were unqualified workers or volunteers).

1.   *Lack of training and knowledge in a new situation*

> *Child abuse disclosure to a volunteer*: a volunteer working in a day centre was approached by a nine-year-old girl with whom she had a good relationship, saying that her father had been hitting her and she was upset. She asked if the volunteer would sit in on a meeting between the girl and her parents. The centre manager encouraged the volunteer to go ahead and provided a room. The volunteer was given no guidance on procedure. She was asked to swear confidentiality by the father at the outset of the meeting. She commented afterwards: 'in my naivety I agreed, which I later found out was a mistake'. She was told about a variety of sexual and physical abuse.

The dilemma here for the volunteer is whether she should respect the confidence and keep her promise to the girl (a

Kantian approach), or break the confidence and discuss the matter with her line manager because of the serious harm that is being done to the girl (a utilitarian approach). A decision may be made by balancing the importance of respecting a confidence against what is in the girl's best interests – weighing up the immediate danger to the girl, and the likelihood of the volunteer being able to persuade the girl to tell someone else. Alternatively the volunteer may realise, or discover, that the agency she works for has a policy that all suspicions about child abuse must be reported to the line manager. She may decide that agency rules should always be followed, or that this particular rule is an important one and it is in the interests of all that it is followed. Therefore the dilemma is resolved and she should tell her line manager.

For the experienced practitioner this case may not present a dilemma at all. First, the experienced practitioner would probably have said at the outset that she could not promise confidentiality. However, assuming she had promised confidentiality because she knew the girl had something important to say and would not be able to say it otherwise, the experienced social worker would usually be much more aware of herself as an employee of an agency and would be familiar with agency rules and procedures and have worked out which ones it was important to follow. She may have worked out from past experience that confidentiality can never be absolute and in her view the best interests of the user always come first.

The learning from this experience for the volunteer was that in similar circumstances next time she would start the meeting by explaining that any information she was given might be shared with the line manager. This might not stop her feeling anxious about sharing the information she was given, but she should not feel guilty about breaking a confidence.

2. Lack of clarity about role

Mother who was working and claiming benefit: a young mother was referred to a family centre because of feelings of social isolation. During a counselling session with her key worker discussing budgeting and the problems caused by spending any time away from her daughter, she revealed that she was claiming income support and working nights as a cleaner. The key worker posed the following questions: 'Should I ignore it? By discussing it with her am I legally condoning it? Should the matter be reported to the DSS? Should the principle of confidentiality be upheld? Is the social worker an agent of the state?'.

This example shows a trainee social worker wondering about the extent to which she is 'an agent of social control' – assuming that her responsibilities to the state extend more widely than they in fact do. She does not realise that if a user has done or is doing something illegal the social worker does not automatically have to report this to the appropriate authority. Usually a social worker would only break confidentiality in these circumstances if a very serious crime was being committed or a life was in danger. While the social worker should not aid and abet a user in an illegal pursuit, discussing the matter does not necessarily entail condoning it. In fact, the social worker can make it clear that what the user is doing is illegal and cannot be condoned.

Not only would the experienced practitioner be clearer about the law, but she would probably have had time to reflect on the complex and contradictory nature of the social worker's role and know when it was appropriate to adopt a social control role, an enabling role or a caring role. She might also ask the question 'whose dilemma is it anyway?' (Bond 1993, p. 191) and realise that it is in fact the user's own ethical dilemma, not the social worker's.

3.   Feeling of lack of confidence in status/position of social worker

Voluntary psychiatric patient: a voluntary patient in a psychiatric hospital suffering from manic depression had her medication changed from oral to injection. The patient objected to this and became aggressive. This was problematic to the nursing staff, as there was a low staff:patient ratio and they were finding her behaviour disruptive. The consultant decided that the injections must be given compulsorily and signed his part of the papers to section her under the Mental Health Act, approaching the hospital social worker at the last minute, regarding her signature as a mere formality. The trainee social worker involved felt this was unjustifiable. But he saw the problems for the social worker involved if she disagreed with the consultant who was in a powerful position.

In this case it is not the trainee social worker who is actually having to make a decision, although if he were, he would regard it as a dilemma – between what the worker regards as the rights and/or best interests of this patient and the importance of maintaining a good relationship with the consultant. In fact, in this case, the social worker does have considerable power as an Approved Social Worker under the Mental Health Act, since her opinion and her signature are required. The trainee social worker may not realise this. It may be the case that the relationship with this particular consultant is difficult, and for an easy life in the future the social worker decides to sign. However, perhaps the social worker does see signing the papers as in the best interests of the patient, given what she knows about the hospital regime and the possibilities of alternative forms of treatment and care.

4. Narrow focus on individual user/one issue

Elderly couple and residential care: Mr and Mrs Finch, aged 91 and 86, were admitted to residential care by the night duty team on a call from the warden of the sheltered accommodation where they lived. They were reported as being unable to cope with everyday domestic functions and Mrs Finch had had a fall in the night. There was pressure from the family, the warden and senior social work colleagues for them to be admitted permanently to residential care. The trainee social worker stated that when she visited them, 'Mr and Mrs Finch were suffering from impaired memory function. They could not comprehend why they had been admitted to residential accommodation, but were categoric that they wanted to return home.' She felt that 'the couple should be allowed to return home on the basis of their individual right to choose'.

The trainee social worker may well be right in this case – that the couple should be allowed to return home – but focussing on their right to choose (a Kantian approach) is only one way of looking at the issue. She might consider the extent to which they are capable of making an informed choice, as well as taking into account the rights and needs of the warden and the family. It seems as though she sees herself principally in the role of advocate for the users, whereas it is often the social worker's job to assess the whole situation and work for a solution in the best interests of all concerned (a more utilitarian approach). In stressing the principle of user self-determination, there appears to be no dilemma here for the trainee social worker. Since she knows what is the morally right course of action, what she feels she is facing is a moral problem – of how to achieve this in the face of opposition. Others might see it as a dilemma – to be resolved by taking various other factors into account, such as, do the users understand the risks attached to returning home; what level of support and responsibility is it fair to place on the warden?

5. *The complexity of the situation is seen, but found to be overwhelming*

> *Banning The Sun newspaper in a residential home*: at a staff meeting at a residential unit for drug users it was decided that the unit should stop buying newspapers published by News International. The reason for this was the dispute at the time between the printers' unions and this publisher. NALGO, the union to which the staff belonged, was supporting a boycott of these papers. The initial ban was just on newspapers from the unit's funds. Subsequently a ban was extended to residents buying *The Sun* out of their own money on the grounds not only of the union dispute, but also its sexist, homophobic and racist stance and its distortions on the subject of AIDS. The trainee social worker reported that 'what initially appeared to be a straightforward dilemma when the ban was introduced as a Union issue soon became a complex and deeply disturbing problem for all concerned'.

The trainee social worker, in writing up this case, raised a series of questions at the end, including asking whether social workers are agents of change, and if so where do the limits of their responsibility to bring about change lie; if *The Sun* is banned, what about television programmes and pornographic magazines; have workers the right to impose their own values on residents? It was only after much reflection and discussion afterwards that this worker came to the view that *The Sun* should not be banned, but rather the issues regarding the dispute with the unions and the prejudiced and offensive nature of much of the material in the newspaper should be discussed with residents. This would entail treating the residents as capable of making their own choices and encouraging them to participate in decision-making.

When is blame and guilt justified? Case studies from practitioners

In experienced practitioners we would generally expect some clarity about their role as social workers, a certain confidence in acting on their own principles, and an ability to hold complexity and contradiction in the work. Nevertheless, even the most experienced practitioners find themselves facing ethical dilemmas, and have feelings of guilt about the choices and actions they take. Some of this guilt and blame is necessary – if we do what we know to be morally wrong, or retreat into defensive practice, or take a decision which turns out to have a bad outcome which we could have predicted if we had thought about it more deeply. Yet some of the guilt and blame is unnecessary and unproductive, as was discussed in chapter 1. It is easy to see how it comes about, for the nature of a dilemma is that whatever decision is made there will be some unwelcome outcomes. Usually there is a choice between two or more conflicting ethical principles, all of which we believe are important. If we can understand that this is the nature of the job, and that, for example, in a particular case, we chose to break confidentiality because another overriding principle relating to the welfare of the user was more important, then we should not regard ourselves as having acted immorally. Rather we have faced up to a difficult ethical decision. The following four case examples relate to two situations where social workers said they felt bad about the decisions they had made and wondered if they should have acted differently, and two situations where the workers knew they had made hard or uncomfortable decisions, but still felt confident that they made the right choice. In the two cases where the workers reported feeling confident about their decisions (one of which also resulted in a bad outcome) both workers felt very clear about where they stood on a particular issue – they had thought through their positions and accepted what the consequences of their actions might be. The four case examples can be categorised as follows (names and some details have been changed to preserve anonymity):

1. The worker felt guilty because a bad outcome occurred and he was aware of the dangers and wondered if he should have done more to prevent this.
2. The worker felt her actions were morally right, despite a bad outcome, because she stuck to a deeply held moral principle.
3. The worker felt guilty because he had to compromise one of his deeply held principles.
4. The worker felt her actions were morally right, despite having to compromise one of her principles, because another principle had priority.

1.   Worker felt guilty about a bad outcome

The following example was given to me by an approved psychiatric social worker, and is a case where the social worker felt he did not act in the user's best interests and felt guilty about this. The fact that there was a bad outcome to the case (the user died) no doubt exacerbated the feelings of guilt.

The user's interests versus the constraints of the agency role. The social worker described a case where he felt the drugs administered by a psychiatrist had caused a patient's physical health to deteriorate, culminating in death by pneumonia. The patient's family were concerned about whether she had been given the right treatment and whether the pnueumonia had been picked up soon enough. The social worker commented: 'I thought it was the drugs that had caused her death. I didn't say it to the family. In the end you're working so much with other health professionals. I colluded.'

The social worker clearly felt quite bad about this case. He had been involved with admitting this woman to hospital originally for 28 days under the Mental Health Act. The social worker felt this was the right decision. On going to hospital she became calmer, accepted her fate and agreed to take medication. But it soon became obvious to the social worker that the medication was affecting her physically. The social worker said he felt responsible for her, as he watched her condition deteriorate as she was shipped backwards and forwards between the psychiatric and general hospitals. He did not seem sure what he could or should have done: 'It is difficult to question consultants. You can only question whether hospital is the best place, not the diagnosis and treatment.'

In hindsight, he suggested that the point at which he could have done something was after the original 28-day section ran out and it was then renewed for six months. He did have a choice at this stage regarding whether to sign the documents as an approved social worker. However, he did feel the patient needed to be in hospital, and trusted the hospital to pick up on any serious physical problems.

This case seems to have three stages: the first stage was the initial committal to hospital which the social worker felt was legally and morally justified. The second stage was the time during the treatment, including the time when the section had to be renewed, when he knew the patient was deteriorating physically, but did not do anything about it. The third stage was after her death when he had to decide whether or not to tell the relatives the truth about his own feelings relating to the cause of death. He commented that with hindsight perhaps he could have acted differently at the second stage, but it would have been difficult. Did he retreat into a kind of defensive practice? He acted within the law and according to agency rules, but was he denying some moral responsibility for the situation when he said that it was not his role to question the diagnosis? It is always a difficult decision to go beyond the agency-defined role – to risk going out on a limb, to challenge another professional when it is not one's role to do so. This is a good example of the type of tough dilemma often faced by social workers, when no course of action has a good outcome. The worker has to try to weigh up how much risk and harm to a patient should be allowed before some action is taken. We can understand the social worker's inaction in this case; perhaps we would not blame him for the patient's death. However, we might think perhaps his own feelings of blame and guilt are justified because he did not do what he thought was in the best interests of the patient. The third stage, where the question of what to say to the relatives arose, is probably less problematic. Given he had signed the papers for the renewal of the section and had not challenged the consultant then or later, he no doubt felt that it was not fair to mention his views about the drugs to the woman's family. The situation might have been different if the social worker had believed the pyschiatrist to be incompetent and likely to put other patients at risk.

2.   *Worker did not feel guilty about bad outcome because she stuck to a deeply-held principle*

The following example was given to me by a youth worker. She felt the case described presented a moral dilemma and she had made a decision based on her belief in confidentiality and user self-determination as absolute moral principles. Although the outcome of the situation was bad, she still felt she had made the morally right decision.

> *Confidentiality and user self-determination versus the user's interests.* The youth worker was working in a busy youth club on a normal youth club evening. She was approached by a 15-year-old girl, Jan, in the coffee bar who was obviously in a state of distress. The youth worker took her into a quiet room. From that initial contact Jan swore the worker to secrecy. Jan revealed to the worker over several weeks that during the past year she had been raped four times by her father and was now pregnant by him. She had also decided to commit suicide as a way out of the situation. The youth worker talked through the issues with Jan, suggesting various options for help and that suicide was not the best way out. However, Jan

continued to refuse to consider any professional help, and insisted that the worker should not tell anyone. The youth worker respected her request for confidentiality. Jan did commit suicide.

Obviously this case relates to a youth worker, not a social worker. If the worker had been working for a social work agency it is highly likely that agency policy would require the worker to report any cases of suspected child abuse and would advise workers not to promise absolute confidentiality. The case would have been analogous to the one given earlier about the volunteer who promised confidentiality. However, in this case it seems there was no agency policy and the worker stuck to the principle of confidentiality because she personally believed it was an important one (a Kantian approach). She did not feel she had any overriding duties to her agency, nor that she should adopt a different set of principles as a youth worker than she should in her everyday life – we might suggest that she was working within the committed practitioner model. She felt that the girl, at 15, was capable of making her own decisions, and should not be treated in a parentalist way. The youth worker, in spite of the girl's suicide, felt she had acted in accordance with her moral principles and therefore her decision not to break the confidence was right.

This is a complex case to explore. For other workers, the decision about whether to break confidence may hardly have presented a dilemma at all. Given it was a case of child abuse and there was even a slight risk of self-inflicted harm to the girl, a line manager or the social services department should have been informed. This would both cover the worker from feeling guilt if the girl did commit suicide, and it would be in the girl's best interests (utilitarian considerations). Others may have seen it as a dilemma, involving the weighing up of the importance of respecting the girl's right to confidentiality and to make her own decisions about her life against the likelihood of the girl committing suicide.

I am less concerned to consider what would have been the 'right' action in this case, and more interested in the fact that this is a situation where a worker apparently did not feel guilty or responsible for a bad outcome. This type of worker is rare in social work, partly because most social workers feel they have a right not to be burdened with the responsibility for someone's death, and they adopt a much more utilitarian approach to moral decision-making by weighing up the possible outcomes of actions and being much more prepared to take a parentalist view of what is in a user's best interests. It is also partly because social work agencies have rules and procedures designed to ensure that an individual worker does not carry the total responsibilty for the outcome of an intervention. Some people may feel that the youth worker should have acted differently and was at least partly to blame for the girl's death. The youth worker was in a position of responsibility in relation to the young people in the club and had a duty to promote their welfare; to adhere rigidly to a personally-held principle of confidentiality may not have been appropriate in this context. Others may feel she was right, seeing her relationship with the girl in the context of a voluntary non-directive counselling role.

3.   Worker felt guilty about compromising a principle

The Manager of a Day Centre for people with learning difficulties described a situation where he felt he had acted 'immorally'. The reason he described his action in this way was because he had made a decision which was contrary to one of the key social work principles that he believed was important for social work – namely, user self-determination.

> *User self-determination versus the interests of the user and others.* John, a 26-year-old man with learning difficulties who had been attending the Day Centre for some time, asked if he could walk to the centre on his own, rather than use the minibus provided by the Social Services Department. Staff of the centre judged that he was capable of doing so, and they thought that this would help him develop his life skills, self-confidence and independence. However, John's parents were extremely worried at this suggestion, feeling that John would not be able to cope. They stated categorically that they

would not allow John to attend the centre if he had to make his own way there. The Centre Manager reluctantly agreed that John should continue to use the bus.

When the social worker who had been the Centre Manager was asked why he came to this decision, it became obvious that he was taking into account the views and feelings of John's parents, as well as what he thought would promote greater self-determination for John. He had weighed up the consequences for John and his parents of insisting that John should walk to the Day Centre. Given that John relied on his parents for care, they had a right to have their views heard. Also it would not be in John's long-term interests if he stopped coming to the Day Centre or if his parents were excessively anxious. So this social worker had in effect gone through a process of weighing up the outcomes of the proposed change as against the status quo and decided that the least harm would be done if the status quo was retained. This social worker did not act 'unethically' – far from it – he actually went through a very serious process of moral reasoning to come to the decision he did. What his decision shows is that the principle of user self-determination is not the only ethical principle, or even the paramount ethical principle for social work practice. Other principles such as promoting the good of the user (which involves other things than self-determination) and promoting the general good (which involves people other than just the user) are also important. If we accept utilitarianism as a theory of ethics, then these are ethical principles. This social worker was facing an ethical dilemma involving a conflict between ethical principles – user self-determination versus the promotion of the greatest good of the greatest number. In order to resolve the dilemma he had to make a choice – and whichever choice he made would go against one of the principles. So it was not surprising that he was left feeling dissatisfied with the outcome. However, should he feel guilty that John was not allowed to exercise his freedom to walk to the Day Centre? Surely he should not, provided he felt he had done all he could to persuade and encourage the parents to allow a trial run. He may feel *regret* that John has not been allowed to walk to the centre, but not guilt. By reflecting on this and discussing it, will this worker feel any less guilty in the future? It is hard to say, but if he accepts that user self-determination is not an absolute moral principle, and that therefore it can be morally right to go against that principle, it might make it easier for him to understand the nature of the decisions he has to make.

4.   *Worker did not feel guilty because she clearly prioritised her principles*

This case is about the dilemmas felt by a Black woman working in an Asian women's project where issues of family violence and neglect came up.

> *The needs of Black children versus the 'betrayal' of the Black community.* An Asian woman moved into the area where the project was based from another part of the country. She was on her own, with five children under six years old, having fled a violent husband. She felt isolated as a newcomer, was given little support from the statutory services and found it hard to cope with the children. Her husband followed her and began harassing her. Some Black professionals were providing her with limited support. In the course of her work, the worker at the Asian Women's Project discovered that the woman was locking up her children in her house and going out, either to seek help, or just for a break. The worker discussed this with her, explaining why it was not an appropriate thing to do, and that the children were being put at risk. However, the woman continued to leave her children locked in the house. The worker had to warn the woman that if she continued to leave her children unattended at home she would have to report her to the social services, and the implications of this might be that the children could be taken into care.
>
> Finally the worker decided that she must inform social services because of the potential danger to the children. The worker found this a tough decision to make, because she felt that in the past social services had treated Black women very badly, and had been insensitive to the complexities of cultural and gender issues. She said: 'It was a betrayal of the Black community in a sense. In the past I had campaigned about the insensitivity of social services. But on this occasion I felt I had to do it because of the risk to the children.'

The worker in this case said she did not feel guilty about what she had done. She felt it was the right decision. Having explained to the woman on several occasions that she should not leave the children on their own and having worked with her trying to sort out her domestic and financial problems, she had given the woman due warning. This seems to be a case where the worker felt regret, but not guilt.

This case highlights some of the tensions felt by Black workers in a professional position. This worker commented on how a large part of her job was trying to explain to the Asian women the British laws, and the powers and roles of the various authorities and services. The women often found it hard to comprehend that neglect of and violence towards children was illegal. The social services and other agencies generally were insensitive to the needs of the Asian women, and were unwilling, or unable, to take into account the whole picture of a woman's life, including her religion and cultural background. The workers at the Asian Women's Project were in a sense mediating between the western and Asian cultures and values. Often their role was resented by members of the Asian community, particularly the men. The workers in the Asian Women's Project were concerned not just about balancing the needs and interests of different sections of the Black community, but also about trying to adopt a committed/radical approach to practice and to work from a Black feminist perspective. This particular worker commented that it was important for her to be very clear about her own values and about her professional commitments. Whilst she had a strong commitment to help the Asian community, she was not prepared to cover up or ignore cases of family violence or neglect where women or children were at risk of harm. She said that she rarely felt guilt or self-blame about the actions she had taken, since she was clear where she stood. Some Black workers who were more ambivalent about their professional roles, particularly statutory social workers seemed to have a tougher time.

Ethical decision-making

All the above cases relate to whether or not a social worker should have felt blame or guilt about the outcomes of her decisions or actions. We have argued that it is important that social workers come to a considered decision. In chapter 1 it was suggested that making a moral judgement should be regarded as an essentially rational process, which can be justified by the social worker. I will end the book by giving just one example of a social work case and analysing how a decision might be made. It involves the classic social work dilemma of deciding whether to promote user self-determination as opposed to acting in what is thought to be the best interests of the user and other interested parties. Discussion of the case raises questions which have been much debated in medicine concerning the principle of informed consent, and how to judge whether someone is capable of understanding what is going on and making a decision (Gillon 1985; Buchanan and Brock 1989; Wicclair 1991). This is an area that could usefully be further explored and developed in social work.

> *The rights of a psychiatric patient: parentalism versus informed choice.* Sylvia, a woman with Huntingdon's disease, had to be moved from a pyschiatric hospital because of shortage of beds. Routine was very important to her, and at first she had found it hard to cope in the hospital, where she had been living for the past six months. A social worker completed a needs assessment with Sylvia's husband and the nursing staff without Sylvia's involvement or knowledge as the nursing staff and husband felt this would disturb her too much. A nursing home was found for her, and the social worker wanted Sylvia to be involved in discussions about the move and to visit the home first. Sylvia's husband and the nursing staff thought this would seriously distress Sylvia, who found it hard to understand what was being said anyway. They thought it would be best for all concerned if she were simply put into a car and taken to the new home without any discussion or prior warning. What should the social worker do?

Ethical issues involved

1. *User's rights to choose and to be informed* – the Kantian principle of respect for persons entails that a user should make decisions about her own life provided she is capable of rational and self-determining action. An important question in this case is to what extent Sylvia is capable of understanding the issues involved, and hence should she have been involved in the choice of the home, or at least be informed in advance about the move?

2. *The user's interests* – what are the user's best interests? The principle of promoting user welfare arises here and the question of whether we take account of the user's own view of her welfare or what others think is best for her (parentalism).

3. *The rights and interests of others* – who are the other parties involved (husband, nurses, the hospital as a public institution) and what are their rights and interests? The utilitarian principle of promoting the greatest good of the greatest number comes in here – which entails questions of distributive justice.

4. *Structural inequalities* – why is Sylvia having to move? How does government policy and power structures in society oppress people with psychiatric problems?

How the issues arose

These issues arose because it was questionable to what extent Sylvia was capable of understanding what was going on and able to make informed decisions and choices. It was therefore possible for parentalist approaches to be argued for. She was also dependent on the care of others and therefore their views and interests had to be taken into account. Changes in government policy meant that beds were no longer available in the psychiatric hospital, and social services rather than the health service must take responsibility for this user. People with pyschiatric problems are not regarded as a high priority in society and tend to be marginalised.

Lines of argument

There are a number of lines of argument that might be pursued by the social worker in coming to a decision and justifying it.

1.   Is the user capable of rational thought and self-determined action? If she is, then it could be argued that she has a right to be involved in the decision about the move – not just to be informed in advance, but to choose whether she wishes to go to that particular nursing home. However, it does not seem clear how much Sylvia understands. She is obviously thought to understand enough to be distressed about the thought of the move. Yet if she is so distressed, is she capable of making an informed choice about whether she wants to go to the nursing home suggested?

In the context of medicine and patients' consent to treatment the principle of 'informed consent' is widely accepted. According to this, patients' decision-making capacity is judged according to whether they have a capacity to understand and communicate, to reason and deliberate and whether they possess a set of values and goals (Wicclair 1991). Not surprisingly, there is no single, universally accepted standard of decision-making capacity. This is not only because medical professionals' judgements about what constitutes a capacity to understand and reason will vary, but also because the levels of competence required will vary according to what type of decision is being made. Buchanan and Brock (1989) suggest that the relevant criteria should vary according to the risk to the patient's well-being. If the treatment is relatively low risk, then a weaker standard of decision-making capacity is appropriate. These are debated issues (see Wicclair 1991; Brock 1991), but are of relevance to the issue of user choice in social work.

It could be argued in this case that giving the user a choice about whether to go to a particular nursing home did not require a strong decision-making capacity and therefore she should be informed and have a choice. However, the question arises as to whether there is really a choice to give Sylvia. She has to move out of the hospital. She is not a consumer paying for a bed of her choice, but a patient subject to the resource allocation decisions of hospital managers. The only choice will be whether she wishes to go to the nursing home offered, or a different one, or to have an alternative system of care. In a case like this it might be appropriate for an independent advocate to work with Sylvia on these issues. For although the social worker may want to give Sylvia some choice, if Sylvia refuses the proposed nursing home, this will involve more work for the social worker in finding alternatives. Brandon (1991, p. 118) argues that it is always preferable to have an independent advocate working on behalf of psychiatric patients:

> The advocate nurse, social worker or doctor has an inherent and critical conflict of interest. The alleged oppressor pays their salaries.

If it is thought that Sylvia is not capable of making any informed decisions, then we might consider applying the principle of substituted judgement which would entail considering what she would have wanted based on our knowledge of her before she became ill (Penhale 1991). This is not a very satisfactory approach since we would not only have to rely largely on the husband's views of his wife's preferences, but his views about what kind of nursing home she might have chosen for herself knowing that she had Huntingdon's disease, and whether she would have preferred to have been told in advance and suffered distress or simply to have been moved. Although it is probably a helpful maxim to consider the situation from the user's point of view, the substituted judgement approach is still very subjective and hypothetical.

2. *What is in the user's best interests?* – at the end of the day it is probably more practical and honest for the people involved in making the decision to consider what *they* think is best for this particular person given what they know about her attitudes and behaviour in the state she is in *now* – that is, a parentalist

approach. Then the arguments of the social worker might be that if Sylvia is talked to about the move, she may feel she is retaining some influence and control over her life and may in fact feel less distress and disorientation as a result of the move. While there may be more distress prior to the move, it may help her settle in better afterwards. The argument of the nursing staff and husband would presumably be that on balance the distress would be greater for Sylvia if she were told.

3.   What would be in the best interests of all the individuals concerned? – if not only Sylvia's well-being but also the interests of the nurses and husband are taken into account, then it could be argued that not to tell Sylvia would make life much easier for the hospital nurses, and perhaps for the husband in the short term. However, if we look to the longer term, and to the interests also of the staff of the new nursing home who will be dealing with a distressed Sylvia by the time she gets there, the social worker could argue that on balance it is in the longer term interests of all concerned if Sylvia is told. The strength of these arguments depends on the confidence we have in the predictions about Sylvia's likely behaviour.

4.   What would bring about changes in attitudes and policies that oppress and disempower psychiatric patients? – the social worker would need to decide whether it was her role, and what she could do to work towards change. This would depend upon the model of social work practice she was operating under, and what time and skills she had. The radical model would suggest that she might discuss the broader policy issues with the consultant and other professionals, publicise the problems in the media and/or work with campaigning groups to raise awareness and change policies.

The social worker's decision

In fact, the social worker in this case decided to ask for a meeting of the nurses, husband and consultant psychiatrist. The psychiatrist agreed with the social worker that Sylvia had a right to know what was going on, although did not feel it was appropriate for her to visit the home. In the end a compromise was reached whereby Sylvia was told of the plans, but she was not allowed to visit the home first. This was the only person with Huntingdon's disease the social worker had worked with. The social worker commented:

> It was a compromise. I would have liked to have taken her to see the nursing home, regardless of whether she knew what was going on. The psychiatrist said that families have their own ways of dealing with things. I felt that as professionals we have to be honest and open with our clients.

The social worker said afterwards that she saw her role as acting in the user's best interests: 'she had a right to know; a right to that distress; we owed it to her to prepare her for the move'. There may have been both Kantian (user's rights) and utilitarian (making things easier) reasons for the social worker's recommendations, although her stress was on the user's rights. Interestingly the social worker did not seem to feel it was important to make a definitive judgement about whether or not the user could be regarded as capable of understanding what was going on, she wanted to treat her as a person regardless. This was probably linked to the social worker's strong sense of her professional duty – 'professionals have to be honest and open' – as opposed to the family's preference for deception. Because the social worker was in effect an outsider, she could take on the role of advocate for the user's rights. She need not, however, have based her view purely on an adherence to the principle of user self-determination. She could have also weighed up the severity of the distress that would be caused by Sylvia being told about the move in advance and how much harm this would actually cause to the nurses, husband and Sylvia herself. Since it was unlikely to be greater than Sylvia's distress at suddenly finding herself in a new home without warning, the social worker could also have argued from a utilitarian point of view that no greater harm would be produced by following her approach.

The social worker in talking about this case was aware of how the situation of Sylvia having to move had arisen (through changes in government policy), but did not mention any action taken to challenge this. For most social workers the day to day work leaves little time or strength to challenge broader structural inequalities and injustices. This social worker was clear about her role as a defender of the user's interests and rights and had the confidence to challenge close family and nursing staff in defence of these principles. It is not always possible for social workers to do this because of their role in working for an agency and needing to preserve good relationships with psychiatrists, for example. This is where the role of an independent advocate becomes important.

Conclusions

Discussion of these case examples shows the importance of critical reflection on social work practice and the need to understand the complexities and contradictions inherent in the role of social worker. This enables social workers to understand more clearly how and why ethical problems and dilemmas arise in practice, and may enable them to be better able to defend themselves and the profession from moral attack and reduce some of the feelings of guilt, blame and anxiety in making difficult ethical decisions. Trainee social workers in particular experience a lot of confusion and anxiety about their roles, which can be reduced through reflection on ethical and value issues and relating them to social work theory and practice.

The rapid changes taking place in the structure and organisation of social work services mean that it is even more important for practitioners to be clear about their value positions in order to resist the authoritarian, bureaucratising trends. These not only threaten professional identity and the traditional values based on respect for individual persons, but make increasingly difficult more radical forms of practice which challenge both the traditional Kantian values and the utilitarian principles of the bureaucratic model.

Exercise 5

Aims of the exercise – to encourage the reader to analyse her/his practice in terms of the ethical issues involved.

Using the format adopted for analysing the last case example in chapter 7:

1. Briefly describe an ethical dilemma experienced in your practice.
2. What were the ethical issues involved?
3. How did they arise?
4. What line of argument would you use to justify the course of action you took?

References

Abbott, P. and Wallace, C. (1990) 'The Sociology of the Caring Professions: An Introduction' in P. Abbott and C. Wallace (eds) *The Sociology of the Caring Professions*, London, Falmer Press, pp. 1–9.

Ahmad, B. (1990) *Black Perspectives in Social Work*, Birmingham, Venture Press.

Aristotle (1954) *The Nichomachean Ethics of Aristotle*, translated by Sir David Ross, London, Oxford University Press.

Association suisse des assistants sociaux diplômé et des éducateurs spécialisés (1990) *Code de déontologie*, Bern, SBS/ASAS.

Audit Commission (1992) *The Community Revolution: Personal Social Services and Community Care*, London, HMSO.

Australian Association of Social Workers Ltd (1989) *Code of Ethics, By-laws on Ethics*, Hawker, AASW.

Bailey, R. and Brake, M. (eds) (1975) *Radical Social Work*, London, Edward Arnold.

Bamford, T. (1989) 'Discretion and managerialism' in Shardlow, S. (ed.) *The Values of Change in Social Work*, London, Routledge, pp.135–54.

Bamford, T. (1990) *The Future of Social Work*, London, Macmillan.

Banks, S. (1990) 'Doubts, dilemmas and duties: ethics and the social worker' in P. Carter et al. *Social Work and Social Welfare Yearbook 2*, Buckingham, Open University Press, pp. 91–106.

Barclay, P. (1982) *Social Workers, Their Role and Tasks*, London, Bedford Square Press.

Bayley, M. (1989) 'Values in locally based work' in S. Shardlow (ed.) *The Values of Change in Social Work*, London, Tavistock/Routledge, pp. 45–60.

Bell, M. and Sinclair, I. (1993) *Parental Involvement in Initial Child Protection Conferences in Leeds: An External Evaluation*, University of York.

Beresford, P. (1984) *Patch in Perspective, Decentralising and Democratising Social Services*, London, Battersea Community Action.

Berry, L. (1988) 'The Rhetoric of Consumerism and the Exclusion of Community', *Community Development Journal*, vol. 23, no. 4, pp. 266–72.

Biestek, F. (1961) *The Casework Relationship*, London, Allen and Unwin.

Bloxham, S. (1993) 'Managerialism in Youth and Community Work: A Critique of Changing Organisational Structures and Management Practice', *Youth & Policy,* No. 41, pp. 1–12.

Bond, T. (1993) *Standards and Ethics for Counselling in Action*, London, Sage.

Brake, M. and Bailey, R. (eds) (1980) *Radical Social Work and Practice*, London, Edward Arnold.

Brandon, D. (1976) *Zen in the Art of Helping*, London, Routledge & Kegan Paul.

Brandon, D. (1991) *Innovation without Change? Consumer Power in Psychiatric Services*, Basingstoke, Macmillan.

Braye, S. and Preston-Shoot, M. (1992) *Practising Social Work Law,* Basingstoke, Macmillan.

British Association for Counselling (1992) *Code of Ethics and Practice for Counsellors*, Rugby, BAC.

British Association of Social Workers (1980) *Clients are Fellow Citizens*, Birmingham, BASW.

British Association of Social Workers (1983) *Effective and Ethical Recording*, Birmingham, BASW.

British Association of Social Workers (1986) *A Code of Ethics for Social Work*, Birmingham, BASW.

British Association of Social Workers (1989) *Rights, Responsibilities and Remedies*, Birmingham, BASW.

Brock, D. (1991) 'Decisionmaking competence and risk', *Bioethics*, vol. 5, no. 2, pp. 105–112.

Brookfield, S. (1987) *Developing Critical Thinkers*, Milton Keynes, Open University Press.

Brown, H. and Smith, H. (1992) 'Assertion not assimilation: a feminist perspective on the normalisation principle' in H. Brown and H. Smith (eds) *Normalisation: A reader for the nineties*, London, Routledge, pp. 149–171.

Buchanan, A. and Brock, D. (1989) *Deciding for Others: The Ethics of Surrogate Decision Making*, Cambridge, Cambridge University Press.

Butrym, Z. (1976) *The Nature of Social Work*, London, Macmillan.

Campbell, T. (1978) 'Discretionary rights' in N. Timms and D. Watson (eds) *Philosophy in Social Work*, London, Routledge and Kegan Paul.

Canadian Association of Social Workers (1983) *Code of Ethics,* Canada, CASW.

Central Council for Education and Training in Social Work (1976) *Values in Social Work*, London, CCETSW.

Central Council for Education and Training in Social Work (1989) *Requirements and Regulations for the Diploma in Social Work*, London, CCETSW.

Chamberlain, L. (1992) 'Right to see the record', *Community Care*, 22 October, pp. 14–15.

Clark, C. with Asquith, S. (1985) *Social Work and Social Philosophy*, London, Routledge & Kegan Paul.

Cohen, P. (1990) 'Anyone for a General Council' '*Social Work Today*, 3 May, pp. 22–4.

Colegio de Asistentes Sociales del Peru (1990) *Código de Ética Profesional*, Lima, CASP.

Collegi Oficial de Diplomats en Treball Social y Assistents Socials de Catalunya (1988) *Codi d'ética dels Assistents Socials: Código de ética de los Asistentes Sociales*, Barcelona, CODTSASC.

Cooper, D. (1993) *Child Abuse Revisited: Children, Society and Social Work*, Buckingham, Open University Press.

Corden, J. and Preston-Shoot, M. (1987) *Contracts in Social Work*, Aldershot, Gower.

Corrigan, P. and Leonard, P. (1978) *Social Work Practice Under Capitalism: A Marxist Approach*, London, Macmillan.

Counsel and Care (1992) *From home to a home*, London, Counsel and Care.

Cranston, M. (1976) 'Human rights, real and supposed' in N. Timms and D. Watson (eds) *Talking About Welfare*, London, Routledge & Kegan Paul, pp. 133–44.

Croft, S. and Beresford, P. (1989) 'Decentralisation and the personal social services' in M. Langan and P. Lee (eds) *Radical Social Work Today*, London, Unwin Hyman, pp. 97–121.

Curnock, K. and Hardicker, P. (1979) *Towards Practice Theory: Skills and Methods in Social Assessments*, London, Routledge & Kegan Paul.

Dalley, G. (1992) 'Social welfare ideologies and normalisation: links and conflicts' in H. Brown and H. Smith (eds) *Normalisation: A reader for the nineties*, London, Routledge, pp. 100–111.

Dalrymple, J. (1993) 'Advice, advocacy and representation for children', *Childright*, July, no. 98, pp. 11–13.

Day, L. (1992) 'Women and oppression: race, class and gender' in M. Langan and L. Day (eds) *Women, Oppression and Social Work*, London, Routledge, pp.12–31.

Department of Health (1988) *Protecting Children: A Guide for Social Workers undertaking a Comprehensive Assessment*, London, HMSO.

Department of Health Social Services Inspectorate (1991a) *Care Management and Assessment: Managers' Guide*, London, HMSO.

Department of Health Social Services Inspectorate (1991b) *Care Management and Assessment: Practitioners' Guide*, London, HMSO.

Dominelli, L. (1988) *Anti-Racist Social Work*, Basingstoke, Macmillan.

Dominelli, L. and McLeod, E. (1989) *Feminist Social Work*, Basingstoke, Macmillan.

Downie, R. (1971) *Roles and Values*, London, Methuen.

Downie, R. and Calman, K. (1987) *Healthy Respect: Ethics in Health Care*, London, Faber & Faber.

Downie, R. and Loudfoot, E. (1978) 'Aim, skill and role in social work' in N. Timms and D. Watson (eds) *Philosophy in social work*, London, Routledge & Kegan Paul, pp. 111–26.

Downie, R. and Telfer, E. (1969) *Respect for Persons*, London, Routledge & Kegan Paul.

Downie, R. and Telfer, E. (1980) *Caring and Curing*, London, Methuen.

Durham County Advocacy Project (1993) *"Speaking Up" in County Durham: First Steps in Developing Advocacy*, Durham, DCAP.

England, H. (1986) *Social Work as Art*, London, Allen & Unwin.

Etzioni, A. (1969) *The Semi-Professions and their Organisation*, New York, The Free Press.

Farley, M. (1993) 'Feminism and Universal Morality' in G. Outka and J. Reeder (eds) *Prospects for a Common Morality*, Chichester, Princeton University Press.

Feinberg, J. (1973) *Social Philosophy*, Englewood Cliffs, New Jersey, Prentice-Hall.

Franklin, B. (1989) 'Wimps and bullies: press reporting of child abuse' in P. Carter et al. (eds) *Social Work and Social Welfare Yearbook*, Milton Keynes, Open University Press, pp. 1–14.

Freire, P. (1972) *Pedagogy of the Oppressed*, London, Penguin.

Gilligan, C. (1982) *In a Different Voice: Psychological Theory and Women's Development*, Cambridge, Mass., Harvard University Press.

Gillon, R. (1985) 'Autonomy and consent' in M. Lockwood (ed.) *Moral Dilemmas in Modern Medicine*, Oxford, Oxford University Press, pp. 111–25.

Goldstein, H. (1981) *Social Learning and Change: a Cognitive Approach to Human Services*, Columbia, South Carolina, University of South Carolina Press.

Gould, A. (1988) *Conflict and control in welfare policy: the Swedish experience*, London, Longman.

Greenwood, E. (1957) 'Attributes of a Profession', *Social Work,* vol. 2, no. 3, pp. 44–55.

Gyford, J. (1991) *Citizens, Consumers and Councils*, London, Macmillan.

Hadley, R. and McGrath, M. (eds) (1980) *Going Local: Neighbourhood Social Services*, London, Bedford Square Press/NCVO.

Hadley, R. and McGrath, M. (1984) *When Social Services are Local: the Normanton Experience*, London, Allen & Unwin.

Halmos, P. (1978) *The Faith of Counsellors*, London, Constable.

Hare, R. M. (1952) *The Language of Morals*, Oxford, Clarendon Press.

Hare, R. M. (1963) *Freedom and Reason*, Oxford, Clarendon Press.

Harris, N. (1987) 'Defensive Social Work', *British Journal of Social Work*, 17, pp. 61–9.

Hollis, M. (1977) *Models of Man*, Cambridge, Cambridge University Press.

Hollis, M. and Howe, D. (1990) 'Moral Risks in the Social Work Role: A Response to Macdonald', *British Journal of Social Work*, 20, pp. 547–52.

Hong Kong Social Welfare Personnel Registration Council (1993) *Code of Ethics for Social Workers in Hong Kong*, Hong Kong, HKSWPRC.

Horne, M. (1987) *Values in Social Work*, Aldershot, Hants, Wildwood House.

Howe, D. (1987) *An Introduction to Social Work Theory*, Aldershot, Hants, Wildwood House.

Howe, D. (1991) 'Knowledge, power and the shape of social work practice' in M. Davies (ed.) *The Sociology of Social Work*, London, Routledge.

Howe, D. (1992) 'Child Abuse and the bureaucratisation of social work', *The Sociological Review*, vol. 40, no. 3, pp. 491–508.

Hudson, B. and Macdonald, G. (1986) *Behavioural Social Work: An Introduction*, London, Macmillan.

Hudson, W. (1970) *Modern Moral Philosophy*, London, Macmillan.

Hugman, R. (1991) *Power in Caring Professions*, London, Macmillan.

Illich, I. et al. (1977) *The Disabling Professions*, London, Marion Boyers.

International Federation of Social Workers (1989) *Comparaison des Formations d'Assistants Sociaux dans les Pays Membres de la Communauté Européenne*, Brussels, IFSW.

International Federation of Social Workers (1990) *Social Workers in the European Community: Training-Employment-Perspectives 1992*, Brussels, IFSW.

Irish Association of Social Workers (1986) *Code of Ethics for Social Work Practice*, Dublin, IASW.

Israel Association of Social Workers (1978) *Code of Professional Ethics for the Israeli Social Worker*, Israel, ISASSW.

Ivory, M. (1993) 'Ten year master plan for GSSC registration', *Community Care*, 21 January, no. 950, p. 1.

Jordan, B. (1975) 'Is the client a fellow citizen?', *Social Work Today*, vol. 6, no. 15, pp. 471–5.

Jordan, B. (1989) *The Common Good: Citizenship, Morality and Self-Interest*, Oxford, Blackwell.

Jordan. B. (1990) *Social Work in an Unjust Society*, Hemel Hempstead, Harvester.

Jordan, B. (1991) 'Competencies and Values', *Social Work Education*, vol. 10, no. 1, pp. 5–11.

Kant, I. (1964) *Groundwork of the Metaphysics of Morals*, New York, Harper & Row.

King, M. and Trowell, J. (1992) *Children's Welfare and the Law: The Limits of Legal Intervention*, London, Sage.

Kutchins, H. (1991) 'The Fiduciary Relationship: The Legal Basis for Social Workers' Responsibilities to Clients', *Social Work*, vol. 36, no. 2, pp. 106–13.

Langan, M. (1993) 'New Directions in Social Work' in J. Clarke (ed.) *A Crisis in Care? Challenges to Social Work*, London, Sage/Open University Press, pp. 149–67.

Langan, M. and Lee, P. (eds) (1989) *Radical Social Work Today*, London, Unwin Hyman.

Leighton, N. (1985) 'Personal and professional values – marriage or divorce?' in D. Watson (ed.) *A Code of Ethics for Social Work: the second step*, London, Routledge & Kegan Paul, pp. 59–85.

Levy, C. (1976) *Social work ethics,* New York, Human Sciences Press.

Levy, C. (1993) *Social Work Ethics on the Line*, Binghampton, New York, The Haworth Press.

Lister, R. (1991) 'Citizenship engendered', *Critical Social Policy,* no. 32, pp. 65–71.

Lukes, S. (1987) *Marxism and Morality*, Oxford, Oxford University Press.

McBeath, G. and Webb, S. (1990–1) 'Child Protection Language as Professional Ideology in Social Work', *Social Work & Social Sciences Review*, 2 (2), pp. 122–45.

McDermott, F. (1975) 'Against the persuasive definition of self-determination' in F. McDermott (ed.) *Self-Determination in Social Work*, London, Routledge & Kegan Paul, pp. 118–37.

Macdonald, G. (1990) 'Allocating Blame in Social Work', *British Journal of Social Work*, 20, pp. 525–46.

MacIntyre, A. (1982) *After Virtue: A Study in Moral Theory*, London, Duckworth.

Marshall, T. (1963) 'Citizenship and social class' in *Sociology at the Crossroads and Other Essays*, London, Heineman, pp. 67–127.

Marshall, T. (1972) 'Value problems of welfare-capitalism', *Journal of Social Policy*, vol. 1, pp. 15–30.

Marx, K. (1963) *Early Writings* (edited by T. Bottomore), London, Fontana.

Marx, K. and Engels, F. (1969) 'Manifesto of the Communist Party' in L. Feuer, (ed.) *Marx and Engels: Basic Writings on Politics and Philosophy,* Glasgow, Collins/Fontana, pp. 43–82.

Mayer, J. and Timms, N. (1970) *The Client Speaks*, London, Routledge & Kegan Paul.

Mill, J. S. (1972) *Utilitarianism, On Liberty, and Considerations on Representative Government*, London, Dent.

Millerson, G. (1964) *The Qualifying Associations: A Study in Professionalisation*, London, Routledge & Kegan Paul.

Mintzberg, H. (1979) *The Structuring of Organisations*, Englewood Cliffs, Prentice Hall.

Moffet, J. (1968) *Concepts of Casework Treatment*, London, Routledge & Kegan Paul.

Morales, A. and Sheafor, B. (1986) *Social Work: A Profession of Many Faces*, Boston, Allyn & Bacon.

Moon, D. (1988) 'Introduction: Responsibility, Rights and Welfare' in D. Moon (ed.) *Responsibility, Rights and Welfare: The Theory of the Welfare State*, Boulder, Colorado, Westview Press, pp. 1–15.

Mullender, A. and Ward, D. (1991) *Self-Directed Groupwork: Users Take Action for Empowerment*, London, Whiting & Birch.

Nagel, T. (1976) 'Moral Luck' '*Proceedings of the Aristotelian Society*, Supplementary, volume L, pp. 137–51.

National Association of Social Workers (1990) *Code of Ethics*, Washington, NASW.

National Consumer Council (1993) *Getting Heard and Getting Things Changed*, London, NCC.

Newcastle upon Tyne Community Care Plan (1993), Newcastle, Newcastle City Council, Newcastle Health Authority, Newcastle Family Health Services Authority.

Newcastle upon Tyne Social Services Department (no date, draft in operation in 1993) *Policy and Procedure in Relation to Access to Information*, Newcastle, Newcastle City Council.

Newell, P. (1991) *The UN Convention and Children's Rights in the UK*, London, National Children's Bureau.

Norman, R. (1983) *The Moral Philosophers*, Oxford, Clarendon Press.

Norwegian Association of Social Workers (NOSO) (1993) *Declaration on Ethical Principles in Social Work*, Oslo, NOSO.

O'Connor, J. (1973) *The Fiscal Crisis of the State*, New York, St Martin's Press.

Offe, C. (1984) *Contradictions of the Welfare State*, London, Hutchinson.

Outka, G. and Reeder, J. (eds) (1993) *Prospects for a Common Morality*, Chichester, Princeton University Press.

Parsons, T. (1959), 'The Professions and Social Structure' in *Essays in Social Theory,* New York, Free Press.

Parton, N. (1989) 'Child abuse' in B. Kahan (ed.) *Child Care Research, Policy and Practice*, London, Hodder & Stoughton/Open University.

Parton, N. (1991) *Governing the Family: Child Care, Child Protection and the State*, Basingstoke, Macmillan.

Parton, N. and Small, N. (1989) 'Violence, social work and the emergence of dangerousness' in M. Langan and P. Lee (eds) *Radical Social Work Today*, London, Unwin Hyman, pp. 120–39.

Payne, M. (1989) 'Open Records and Shared Decisions with Clients' in Shardlow, S. (ed.) *The Values of Change in Social Work*, London, Routledge, pp. 114–34.

Payne, M. (1991) *Modern Social Work Theory: a critical introduction*, Basingstoke, Macmillan.

Penhale, B. (1991) 'Decision-making and mental incapacity: practice issues for professionals', *Practice,* vol. 5, no. 3, pp. 186–95.

Pincus, A. and Minahan, A. (1973) *Social Work Practice: Model and Method*, Itasca, Illinois, Peacock.

Pinker, R. (1990) *Social Work in an Enterprise Society*, London, Routledge.

Plamenatz, J. (1966) *The English Utilitarians*, Oxford, Blackwell.

Plant, R. (1970) *Social and Moral Theory in Casework*, London, Routledge and Kegan Paul.

Poole, R. (1991) *Morality and Modernity,* London, Routledge.

Ragg, N. (1977) *People not Cases,* London, Routledge and Kegan Paul.

Ramon, S. (ed.) (1991) *Beyond Community Care: Normalisation and Integration Work*, London, Macmillan.

Raphael, D. (1981) *Moral Philosophy*, Oxford, Oxford University Press.

Rawls, J. (1972) *A Theory of Justice,* Oxford, Clarendon Press.

Rhodes, M. (1986) *Ethical Dilemmas in Social Work Practice,* Boston, Mass., Routledge and Kegan Paul.

Rice, D. (1975) 'The Code: a voice for approval', *Social Work Today*, 18 October, pp. 381–2.

Rickford, F. (1992) 'Action stations', *Social Work Today*, 28 May, pp. 10–11.

Roberts, R. (1990) *Lessons from the Past: Issues for Social Work Theory*, London, Routledge.

Rogers, C. (1951) *Client-Centred Therapy: its Current Practice, Implications and Theory*, London, Constable.

Rogers, C. (1961) *On Becoming a Person: a Therapist's View of Psychotherapy*, London, Constable.

Rojeck, C. and Collins, S. (1987) 'Contract or Con Trick', *British Journal of Social Work*, 17, pp. 199–211.

Rojeck, C. and Collins, S. (1988) 'Contract or Con Trick Revisited', *British Journal of Social Work*, 18, pp. 611–22.

Ronnby, A. (1992) 'Praxiology in social work', *International Social Work*, vol. 35, pp. 317–26.

Ronnby, A. (1993) 'The Carer Society & Ethics', unpublished paper, Department of Social Work & Humanities, Mid-Sweden University, Östersund.

Sartre, J-P. (1969) *Being and Nothingness,* London, Methuen.

Schön, D. (1983) *The Reflective Practitioner: How Professionals Think in Action*, New York, Basic Books.

Schön, D. (1987) *Educating the Reflective Practitioner. Towards a New Design for Teaching and Learning in the Professions*, San Francisco, Jossey-Bass.

Shah, N. (1989) 'It's up to you sisters: black women and radical social work' in M. Langan and P. Lee (eds) *Radical Social Work Today*, London, Unwin Hyman, pp. 178–91.

Smart, J. and Williams, B. (1973) *Utilitarianism, For and Against*, Cambridge, Cambridge University Press.

Smith, M. (1994) *Local education: Community, conversation, praxis*, Buckingham, Open University Press.

Spicker, P. (1988) *Principles of Social Welfare*, London, Routledge.

Stalley, R. (1978) 'Non-judgmental attitudes' in N. Timms and D. Watson (eds) *Philosophy in Social Work*, London, Routledge & Kegan Paul.

Stevenson, L. (1974) *Seven Theories of Human Nature*, Oxford, Oxford University Press.

Strawson, P. (1959) *Individuals*, London, Methuen.

Swedish Union of Social Workers, Personnel & Public Administrators (SSR) (1991) *Guidelines for Professsional Ethics in Social Work*, Stockholm, SSR.

Taylor, D. (1989) 'Citizenship and social power', *Critical Social Policy*, 26, pp. 19–31.

Taylor, D. (1991/2) 'A Big Idea for the nineties? the rise of the citizens' charters', *Critical Social Policy*, 33, pp. 87–94.

Thomas, T. et al. (1993) *Confidentiality in Social Services*, London, CCETSW.

Thompson, I. et al. (eds) (1988) *Nursing Ethics*, Edinburgh, Churchill Livingstone.

Thompson, N. (1993) *Anti-Discriminatory Practice*, Basingstoke, Macmillan.

Toren, N. (1972) *Social Work: The Case of a Semi-Profession*, Beverley Hills, Sage.

Tronto, J. (1993) *Moral Boundaries: A Political Argument for an Ethic of Care*, London, Routledge.

United Nations (1959) *Declaration of the Rights of the Child*, reprinted in P. Newell, *The UN Convention and Children's Rights in the UK*, London, National Children's Bureau, pp. 182–3.

von Bertalanffy, L. (1971) *General System Theory: Foundations, Development, Application*, London, Allen Lane.

Vernon, S. (1993) *Social Work and the Law*, London, Butterworths.

Warnock, G. (1967) *Contemporary Moral Philosphy*, London, Macmillan.

Watson, D. (1985) 'What's the point of A Code of Ethics for Social Work' in D. Watson (ed.) *A Code of Ethics for Social Work: the second step*, London, Routledge & Kegan Paul, pp. 20–39.

Whitley, C. (1969) 'On duties' in J. Feinberg (ed.) *Moral Concepts*, Oxford, Oxford University Press, pp. 53–9.

Wicclair, M. (1991) 'Patient decision-making capacity and risk', *Bioethics*, vol. 5, no. 2, pp. 91–104.

Wilding, P. (1982) *Professional Power and Social Welfare*, London, Routledge & Kegan Paul.

Wilkes, R. (1981) *Social Work with Undervalued Groups*, London, Tavistock.

Wilkes, R. (1985) 'Social work: what kind of profession?' in D. Watson (ed.) *A Code of Ethics for Social Work: the second step*, London, Routledge and Kegan Paul, pp. 40–58.

Winch, P. (1958) *The Idea of a Social Science and its Relation to Philosophy*, London, Routledge & Kegan Paul.

Wittgenstein, L. (1967) *Philosophical Investigations*, Oxford, Blackwell.

Index

177